A beginner's guide to foreign exchange success

Forex
made simple

Kel Butcher

Wrightbooks

First published 2011 by Wrightbooks
an imprint of John Wiley & Sons Australia, Ltd
42 McDougall Street, Milton Qld 4064

Office also in Melbourne

Typeset in 11.5/13.4 pt Berkeley

National Library of Australia Cataloguing-in-Publication data:

Author:	Butcher, Kel.
Title:	Forex made simple: a beginner's guide to foreign exchange success / Kel Butcher.
ISBN:	9780730375241 (pbk.)
Notes:	Includes index.
Subjects:	Foreign exchange.
	Foreign exchange market.
	Foreign exchange futures.
	Investments—Computer network resources.
	Electronic trading of securities.
Dewey Number:	332.45

Cover design by Peter Reardon
Pipeline Design <www.pipelinedesign.com.au>

Printed in Australia by Ligare Book Printer

10 9 8 7 6 5 4 3 2 1

Disclaimer
The material in this publication is of the nature of general comment only, and does not represent professional advice. It is not intended to provide specific guidance for particular circumstances and it should not be relied on as the basis for any decision to take action or not take action on any matter which it covers. Readers should obtain professional advice where appropriate, before making any such decision. To the maximum extent permitted by law, the author and publisher disclaim all responsibility and liability to any person, arising directly or indirectly from any person taking or not taking action based upon the information in this publication.

Contents

The secret of success is constancy of purpose.
Benjamin Disraeli

About the author

Kel Butcher is a private trader, entrepreneur and investor. Kel has more than 20 years' experience in financial markets, trading shares, futures, options, warrants and CFDs. He works as a consultant to a managed fund, a boutique trading company and a share-trading software developer. Kel is a regular contributor to *YourTradingEdge* magazine and is the author of *A Step-by-Step Guide to Buying and Selling Shares Online* and *20 Most Common Trading Mistakes and How You Can Avoid Them*. He also featured in *The Wiley Trading Guide*.

Passionate about money management, risk management and position-sizing techniques, Kel acts as a mentor and coach to fellow traders. He can be contacted by email at <kel@tradingwisdom.com.au>.

When he's not trading, Kel enjoys snowboarding, mountain bike riding and surfing. He lives on the NSW Central Coast with his wife Cate and his two sons Jesse and Ollie.

Acknowledgements

My thanks as always go to the staff at Wrightbooks, and in particular Kristen Hammond, for all the help and support in getting this book from concept to book in a short space of time. I would also like to thank FXCM for the use of various screen shots in this book. Glen Larson at Genesis FT deserves special mention for the development of the world's best charting program, Trade Navigator.

I am always honoured to be able to write a book and can't do it without the support of my wife, Cate, and my boys, Jesse and Ollie, and the input and shared experiences of the hundreds of traders and other market participants that I have spoken and corresponded with over many years.

Preface

Derived from the words *foreign* and *exchange*, forex (often abbreviated simply to FX) is the practice of trading currencies or money. The foreign exchange market, also referred to as FOREX, Forex, retail forex, FX, margin FX, spot FX or just 'spot', is the largest financial market in the world. Daily trading volumes are approaching US$4 trillion a day — that's more than three times the total of the world's stocks and futures markets combined.

The forex market is an over-the-counter (OTC) market. This means that, unlike stock markets and futures markets, there is no central exchange or specific place where trades occur and orders are matched. Instead, forex dealers and market makers are linked around the globe and around the clock by computer and telephone, creating one huge electronic market place.

Once the domain of the large hedge funds, major corporations and international banks, the forex market has become available to retail traders mostly because of the internet, which has allowed the development and evolution of online trading platforms, so that many firms have been able to open up the foreign exchange market to retail clients.

These online platforms not only allow instant execution into the market, but also provide charts and real-time news services. This allows traders to keep abreast of news unfolding around the globe as it happens. The result has been a huge surge in volume of currencies traded as retail clients become aware of the benefits of trading a market that trades virtually continuously from Monday morning Australian time until early Saturday morning Sydney time.

The forex market allows you to actively engage in online trading using broker platforms to buy and sell currencies. The use of leverage when trading in the forex market means that a small amount of money can be used to control much larger positions than would be possible without the use of leverage. But while leverage can help magnify returns, it also magnifies losses when they occur.

Before throwing yourself head first into real money trading you should take the time to familiarise yourself with the principles of foreign exchange trading and ensure you have a full understanding of how it all works. It is also important to understand the evolution of foreign exchange and some of the key milestones in the development of this market into what it is today. So, let's get started.

chapter 1

History of foreign exchange

The roots of modern-day currency trading can be traced back to the Middle Ages when countries with different currencies began to trade with each other. Payments for these transactions were generally made in gold or silver bullion or coins by weight. Transactions were made through money-changers operating in the major trading centres and market places. Their main roles were to weigh the bullion or coins with a degree of precision and to determine the authenticity of the coins being exchanged.

Over time, a system of transferable bills of exchange evolved for use by traders and merchants, reducing the need for them to carry around large amounts of gold or silver bullion or coins.

Introduction of the gold standard

As economies began to expand and international trade grew, so too did the need to make transactions simpler and add stability to the exchange of currencies around the globe. Payments made using gold and silver were not only cumbersome, but were also affected by price changes caused by shifts in supply and demand.

The Bank of England took the first steps to stabilise its country's currency. The Bank Charter Act of 1844 established Bank of England Notes, which were fully backed by gold, as the legal standard for currency.

In 1857, US banks suspended payments in silver, which it had used since the introduction of a silver standard in 1785, as silver had lost much of its appeal as a store of value. This had a disastrous effect on the financial system and is seen by many as a contributing factor to the American Civil War. In 1861 the US government suspended payments in both gold and silver, and began, through the government central bank, a government monopoly on the issue of new banknotes. This gradually began to restore stability to the country's financial system, as the banknotes began to be accepted as a single store of value — unlike the supply of gold and silver, the supply of these notes could be regulated.

Following the American Civil War, as the US economy expanded and international trade increased, there was a dramatic increase in the demand for credit to facilitate trade and finance rapidly expanding world economies.

The main aim of the implementation of the gold standard, whereby currencies are linked to the price of gold, was to guarantee the value of any currency against that of another. Because countries participating in the gold standard maintained a fixed price for gold, currency exchange rates were thus fixed to the gold price. Each country also had to maintain adequate gold reserves to back its currency's value, which provided a high level of stability.

The British pound, for example, was fixed at £4.2472 per ounce of gold (1 ounce is equal to about 28 grams), while the US dollar was fixed at $20.67 per ounce of gold. So the exchange rate was essentially fixed at US$4.8667 per £1 (US$20.67/£4.2472 = US$4.8667).

Tip

The use of a gold standard to control monetary policy (the use of interest rates to slow or grow an economy) and its impact on inflation, unemployment and economic growth has many economic implications that are beyond the scope of this book.

If the supply of gold remains relatively stable, then so does the supply of money. The use of a gold standard essentially prevents a country from printing too much money, thereby limiting inflation, but at the cost of higher unemployment.

From the perspective of the forex market, the use of a gold standard implies a system of fixed exchange rates between countries. If all countries are on the gold standard, then there is really only one 'real' currency — the price of gold — from which the value of all currencies is determined. The gold standard leads to stability in foreign exchange rates, which is often cited as one of the biggest benefits of using the standard.

The stability that results from use of the gold standard is also one of its biggest drawbacks, because it prevents exchange rates from responding freely to changing circumstances in different countries.

Tip

A gold standard limits the monetary policies a country's central bank can use to stabilise prices and other economic variables, resulting in severe economic shocks.

After a long period of relative stability, the gold standard broke down at the beginning of World War I as the larger European powers were forced to focus their spending on military projects, which led to the printing of excess money. The outbreak of war also interrupted trade flow and the free movement of gold, undermining the ability of the gold standard to function as it should — allowing gold to flow back and forth between countries to ensure a stable currency base.

The gold standard was briefly reinstated between 1925 and 1931 as the Gold Standard Exchange. Facing massive gold and capital outflows as a result of the Great Depression, Britain departed from the gold standard in 1931, and this latest version of the gold standard broke down.

By the mid 1930s London had become the global centre for foreign exchange and the British pound served as the currency both to trade and to keep as a reserve currency. Foreign exchange was originally traded on telex machines, or by cable, earning the pound the nickname *cable*.

Major influences on foreign exchange since World War II

The real growth of the forex market has taken place as a result of events after World War II. The abandonment of the gold standard and the war effort had devastated the British and other European economies. The British pound had also been destabilised by the counterfeiting activities of the Nazis.

In stark contrast to the affects of World War II on the British pound, the US dollar was transformed from a dismal failure after the 1929 stock market collapse, to the leading benchmark currency to which most international currencies were compared. The US economy was on fire. The US emerged as a global economic powerhouse and the US dollar became the pre-eminent global currency.

The Bretton Woods Accord

While the war raged in Europe, representatives of the British and US treasury departments were already planning for postwar economic reconstruction. Central to this was the ability to allow free trade to be conducted without wild currency fluctuations or sudden depreciation, coupled with an effective system of international payments.

During July of 1944 the 44 allied nations met for the United Nations Monetary and Financial Conference at Bretton Woods in the US. The countries agreed to a number of measures designed to stabilise the global economy and currency markets in the aftermath of the war. Chief among these measures was an obligation for each country to adopt a monetary policy that pegged its currency to the US dollar. Each currency was permitted to fluctuate plus or minus 1 per cent from this initial value. When a currency exceeded this range, and at specified predetermined intervention points, the central bank of the country had to either buy or sell the local currency in order to bring it back into the range. This became known as the Bretton Woods system.

As the US dollar was pegged to the value of gold at US$35 per ounce, all currencies were effectively still pegged to the gold price. The US dollar was now assuming the role played by gold under the gold standard. The US dollar became the world's reserve currency.

In order to regulate the member countries' currencies, and to ensure procedures and rules put in place at Bretton Woods were adhered to, the International Monetary Fund (IMF) and International Bank for Reconstruction and Development (IBRD), now the World Bank, were established. The major purpose of the IMF was to maintain a stable system for buying and selling currencies between countries, and to ensure payments for international trade and exchange were conducted in a timely and smooth manner.

The main tasks of the IMF (as noted on its website) were and still are to:

⇨ provide a forum for cooperation on international monetary problems

⇨ facilitate the growth of international trade, thus promoting job creation, economic growth and poverty reduction

⇨ promote exchange rate stability and an open system of international payments

⇨ lend countries foreign exchange when needed, on a temporary basis and under adequate safeguards, to help them address balance of payments problems.

The Nixon Shock

The decision now referred to as the Nixon Shock was a series of measures taken by US president Richard Nixon that destroyed the Bretton Woods system and led to the free-floating currency system that exists today.

By 1970 the cost of the Vietnam War and increased domestic spending were causing a rapid rise in inflation in the United States. The US was also running both a balance of payments deficit and a trade deficit, causing other Bretton Woods member countries to become concerned about America's ability to pay its debts. To cover this spending the US was printing excess money, resulting in a dollar glut. In effect the US dollar was over-valued compared with the other currencies that were part of the Bretton Woods Accord.

At the same time, gold was trading at a higher price on the free market than the rate at which it was pegged against the US dollar. This allowed traders to make an arbitrage play by buying pegged gold with US dollars and selling it at the higher prices prevailing in the free market. This combination of events saw government gold coverage of the US dollar decline from around 56 per cent to less than 25 per cent. When the US lifted its quota on the import of oil, this also triggered further massive dollar outflows from the US economy.

In May 1971 West Germany, fearful of building inflationary pressures in both the German and global economies as a result of the US trade and balance of payments deficit, became the first member country to opt out of the Bretton Woods system, and the value of the US dollar declined by 7.5 per cent against the German (Deutsche) mark. During this period France accumulated almost US$200 million worth of gold, and Switzerland US$50 million of gold, further depleting US gold reserves. In early August 1971, as the US Congress recommended devaluation of the US dollar to protect it from what they referred to as foreign price gougers, Switzerland also withdrew from the Bretton Woods system.

On 15 August 1971 President Richard Nixon announced measures to combat the rampant inflation in the US and stabilise the economy. These included a 90-day price and wages freeze, a 10 per cent import surcharge, and the cancellation of the convertibility of US dollars to gold. These decisions were made without consultation with the other members of the Bretton Woods system, and became known as the Nixon Shock.

Tip

From a foreign exchange trading perspective, the dropping of the gold standard led to the free floating of most major world currencies and opened up the global financial markets.

The Smithsonian Agreement

Despite abandoning the Bretton Woods system, Nixon was still uncertain that the free market could allow a true and fair representation of a currency's value. Like many at the time, he was concerned that an entirely unregulated foreign exchange market could lead to currency devaluations and the breakdown of international trade.

In December 1971 the G10 (Group of 10) countries agreed under the terms of the Smithsonian Agreement to maintain fixed exchange rates without the backing of gold. The G10 countries are Belgium, Canada, France, Germany, Italy, Japan, the Netherlands, Sweden, Switzerland, the United Kingdom and the United States. The US dollar was also to be allowed to float within a 2.25 per cent range, instead of just 1 per cent as under the Bretton Woods system. The free market price of gold exploded to more than $215 per ounce and the US trade deficit continued to grow. In light of these issues and a host of others, the foreign exchange markets were closed in February 1972, and the Smithsonian Agreement collapsed. When the forex markets reopened in 1973 the US dollar was not fixed to any underlying value measure and its value was not confined to within any predetermined valuation parameters.

Floating the dollar, coupled with rising oil prices resulting from conflict in the Middle East at the time, created stagflation in the US economy. Stagflation occurs when unemployment and inflation are both high. The result was the introduction of a range of new economic policies in the US that saw confidence return to the US economy.

Free-floating currencies

The death of the Bretton Woods system and the collapse of the Smithsonian Agreement ultimately led to the system of free-floating currencies that exists today. By 1978 the free floating of currencies was mandated by the IMF. By this time, foreign exchange markets had evolved considerably and allowed a laissez-faire approach to international currency trade. The true free-market nature of this market saw liquidity and volumes continue to grow, making foreign exchange trading more appealing for speculators and hedgers, as well as the traditional users of these markets.

A free-floating currency's value is a function of the current supply and demand forces in the market, rather than a synthetic value created by intervention policies. Free-floating currencies can also be traded openly by all market participants and speculators. Free-floating currencies experience the heaviest trading demand. While a free-floating currency is much easier to trade than a regulated or manipulated currency, liquidity is also a major consideration.

Currency reserves

Before the Bretton Woods Accord, the official means of international payment, and thus the official international reserve, was gold. Under the Bretton Woods system the official reserve currency for the global financial system was the US dollar. Between 1944 and 1968 the US dollar could be converted into gold, and from 1968 to 1973 central banks could convert US dollars into gold, but only from their own official gold reserves.

Since the collapse of the Smithsonian Agreement in 1973, no major currencies have been convertible into gold. Instead, countries and large corporations now hold currency reserves. Reserve currencies, or foreign exchange reserves, are simply assets held in various currencies. Foreign exchange reserves are important indicators of the ability to repay foreign debt and for currency defence, and are used to determine the credit ratings of nations. Holding currency reserves in place of gold reserves led to a significant increase in volumes and liquidity in the foreign exchange markets. As countries and large corporations buy and sell currencies in response to constantly changing economic and geo-political events, this adds huge liquidity to the market.

Currently the euro and Japanese yen are also considered safe-haven currencies during periods of instability. The portfolio of reserve currencies a country or financial institution may hold changes depending on international conditions.

The Swiss franc is often included, but at times this can be problematic because the franc has lower levels of liquidity than the US dollar, euro and Japanese yen. The introduction of the euro currency in 1999 has had the biggest influence on the number of US dollars held as reserve currency. Since 1999 the proportion of US dollars held in official reserve currency by central banks and other financial institutions around the world has dropped from just under 71 per cent to slightly more than 62 per cent, while the euro has risen from just under 18 per cent to 27 per cent.

Tip

The US dollar is still the most widely held reserve currency, and it is considered to have reserve-currency status. The US dollar is still considered a safe haven in times of economic uncertainty and global upheaval, because the US is still seen as a safe economy backed by the US Treasury.

The European Community and the introduction of the euro

More recently, the emergence of the euro currency has had a dramatic impact on foreign exchange markets. An understanding of the events leading up to the release of the euro currency is important for understanding the role of the Eurozone in the global economy and the euro currency in global foreign exchange markets.

The European Monetary Union was created as a result of a long and continuous series of efforts after World War II to create closer economic cooperation among the capitalist European countries. The European Community (EC) commission's officially stated goals were to improve inter-European economic cooperation, create a regional area of monetary stability, and act as 'a pole of stability in world currency markets'. The first steps in this rebuilding were taken in 1950, when the European Payment Union was instituted to facilitate the inter-European settlement of international trade transactions. The purpose of the community was to promote inter-European trade in general, and to eliminate restrictions on the trade of coal and raw steel, in particular, as both were in high demand following the war.

The European Economic Community was established in 1957 under the Treaty of Rome. One of its main objectives was to eliminate customs duties and other barriers that hindered free trade and movement between the member nations. At the same time it began to set up trade barriers against non-member nations.

In 1969 a conference of European leaders set the objective of establishing a monetary union within the EC in order to stimulate European trade and bring together the member nations so they could compete successfully with the growing economies of the United States and Japan. The EC aimed to implement a common European currency by 1980.

In 1978 the then nine members of the EC ratified a new plan for stability—the European Monetary System (EMS). This new system, implemented in 1979, employed an exchange rate mechanism (ERM) to encourage participating countries to maintain their currency exchange rates within a defined range. These permissible limits were derived from the European Currency Unit (ECU). The ECU was a basket of currencies of the European Community member states used as the internal accounting unit within the EC and for some large international financial transactions.

In 1988 a three-stage plan was proposed to allow EU members to reach full economic union, to advance social and economic unity within what became known as the Eurozone, and to increase its presence in the global financial arena. Included in this plan was the establishment of the European Central Bank and a single currency to replace existing national currencies, culminating in full convergence in the Economic and Monetary Union (EMU) or European Monetary Union as it is more generally known. The EMU is essentially the agreement among the member nations to adopt a single currency unit and monetary system. These plans were formalised in the Maastricht Treaty in 1992. In 1993 the European Union (EU) was formally established with 15 member nations.

In 1999, more than 40 years after the idea was first proposed, the euro was introduced as an all-European currency by 11 of the then 15 member states. It remained an accounting-only currency until 1 January 2002, when euro notes and coins were issued and individual national currencies, such as the French franc and the German mark, began to be phased out.

As well as its role in helping create a single European market place, the single euro currency has a number of other benefits, which include:

⇨ the elimination of exchange rates and fees within the Eurozone

⇨ price transparency between countries

⇨ ease of travel for citizens, and goods and services across traditional geographic borders

⇨ lower interest rates

⇨ the formation of a liquid and respected international currency that is used by foreign investors and traders

⇨ the creation of a social and political symbol of integration and unity.

The euro is now used by 16 of the 27 EU members and accounts for more than 25 per cent of global currency reserves. The member states that use the euro as their sole currency are referred to as the Eurozone.

Recent growth of foreign exchange markets

In addition to the historical events that led to the development and evolution of global foreign exchange markets, some more recent events have contributed to the explosion in interest in trading foreign exchange not only among large financial institutions and banks, but also at the retail trader level. Foreign exchange trading has experienced spectacular growth in volume since currencies began to free float in 1978. In 1977, when currencies were still regulated, average daily turnover was around US$5 billion. This had increased to US$600 billion in 1987, and reached the US$1 trillion per day mark in September 1992. Average daily turnover in the forex market is now approaching US$4 trillion—a number that dwarfs all other financial markets. Currency volatility and intra-day price moves are the primary drivers of this explosive growth in volume, and they could never have occurred under a regulated environment.

Some of the main developments that have contributed to the growth of this market include interest rate volatility, international business operations, increased international trade and the use of currency hedging, automated dealing systems, and the internet and retail traders.

Interest rate volatility

Economic globalisation and the increased importance and use of monetary policy have had a significant impact on interest rates. Economies have become much more interrelated, exacerbating the need to change interest rates in response to global economic and geo-political events and to changes in economic conditions between trading partners. Interest rates are altered by the central bank in each country to adjust economic growth and to control inflation. Raising interest rates will slow spending and growth, while lowering interest rates generally leads to more spending and higher growth. Interest-rate differentials between countries affect exchange rates.

Tip

A strong economy with low inflation and interest rates that are high relative to the country's trading partners will experience a rise in its currency's value. An economy that is perceived as being weak, and having low interest rates, will usually have a weaker currency.

The movement of money between countries and currencies to take advantage of these interest-rate differentials is a major contributor to both the volume and volatility of currency trades. The process of buying a high-yield currency (one with a high interest rate) and selling a currency with a low yield (one with a low interest rate) is referred to as a carry trade, which will be discussed in detail in chapter 6.

International business operations

Business globalisation and competition have intensified in parallel with economic globalisation as businesses search for new markets for finished goods, as well as cheaper input costs of labour and raw materials. The pace of internationalisation has expanded in recent decades as a result of a number of major events. These include the fall of communism in the Eastern Bloc countries and the Soviet Union, economic crises in South-East Asia and South America, and the rise of both China and India as global economic powerhouses. These events have influenced the demand and supply of both raw materials and finished goods. As a result, the supply and demand of various currencies during these periods is also affected, as wealth and asset protection measures are implemented at both a corporate and government level.

Increased international trade and the use of currency hedging

The successful handling of foreign exchange transactions and the use of hedging strategies to protect against adverse currency movements, or to lock in either the cost of raw materials or the sale price of finished goods, can affect the profits of businesses involved in the global market place. The profit from the successful sale of a product in overseas markets can be seriously eroded due to adverse foreign exchange movements. Corporate and business interest in foreign exchange transactions and hedging activities has increased in line with increased international trade, adding substantially to the volume of currency transactions undertaken. Many larger businesses and corporations may also participate speculatively in the foreign exchange market in order to profit from trading opportunities, in addition to their hedging activities.

Automated dealing systems

The introduction of automated foreign exchange dealing systems in the 1980s and electronic matching systems in the 1990s had a massive impact on the speed and safety of foreign exchange transactions. Automated online dealing systems link the interbank market electronically, allowing all major participants to be interlinked 24 hours a day and to trade virtually continuously with whoever is in the market at any one time. Automated dealing systems also allow large-volume trades, as well as faster and more reliable simultaneous trades than telephone and telex transactions. These trades are also safer and more transparent, as both parties to the transaction can see exactly what has happened. The electronic matching systems developed and used by brokers have allowed thousands of brokers to access the foreign exchange market and provide foreign exchange trading platforms to their clients. This has opened the foreign exchange market up to a vast number of retail traders and contributed significantly to the rapid expansion in foreign exchange trade volumes over the past 10 years.

The internet and retail traders

Coupled with the development of dealing and matching systems, the advent of the internet has opened up the foreign exchange market to retail traders and others who can now trade online using a broker platform and an internet connection. This has provided access to the foreign exchange market for thousands of speculators and traders, and added a large amount of intra-day speculative volume to the market. Once the domain of the large banks, fund managers and corporations, the foreign exchange market is now accessible to a much wider range of clients using various strategies and methods for trading the markets, and adding to the market's volatility as well as its volume and liquidity. The ongoing education of traders and improvements in the understanding of the foreign exchange markets will continue to add volume to the market as more and more traders are introduced to, and become confident with, trading foreign exchange.

Chapter summary

⇨ The roots of modern-day currency trading can be traced back to the Middle Ages, when trade between countries with different currencies began.

⇨ The main aim of the implementation of the gold standard was to guarantee the value of any currency against that of another.

⇨ The stability that results from the use of the gold standard is also one of its biggest drawbacks, as it prevents exchange rates from responding freely to changing circumstances in different countries. A gold standard also limits the monetary policies that a country's central bank can use to stabilise prices and other economic variables, which can cause severe economic shocks.

⇨ The real growth of the foreign exchange market place has taken place as a result of events occurring after World War II.

⇨ The Bretton Woods Accord established the US dollar as the global currency.

⇨ The death of the Bretton Woods system and the collapse of the Smithsonian Agreement ultimately led to the system of free-floating currencies that exists today. By 1978 the free floating of currencies was mandated by the International Monetary Fund (IMF).

⇨ The creation of the European Monetary Union was the result of a long series of post–World War II efforts aimed at creating closer economic cooperation among the capitalist European countries

⇨ In 1999, more than 40 years after the idea was first proposed, the euro was introduced as an all-European currency by 11 of the then 15 member states.

⇨ Average daily turnover in the foreign exchange market is now approaching the US$4 trillion level—a number that dwarfs the value of trades in all other financial markets.

⇨ Thanks to the advent of the internet and technological advancements in relation to trading platforms and dealing systems, the foreign exchange market can now be traded by a much wider community of traders around the globe and around the clock.

chapter 2

Major currencies, economies and central banks

While you may be itching to start trading, if you are to become a competent and confident forex trader you will need an understanding of the underlying concepts of foreign exchange to give you a solid foundation on which to build your trading business. Understanding the roles and uses of the major (and some of the minor) currencies, the workings of the global economy, and the many interrelationships that exist will help your decision-making processes and the development of your trading system or strategy.

Major world currencies

Although all countries have their own currency, foreign exchange trading is limited to the currencies that have a global presence through their use in international trade and investment. In this chapter, we will look at the seven most actively traded global currencies: the US dollar, the euro, the

Japanese yen, the British pound, the Australian dollar, the Swiss franc and the Canadian dollar.

The United States dollar

The US dollar (USD, $) effectively became the world's reserve currency under the Bretton Woods Accord of 1944. As a result the US dollar is still the world's main currency, and most global trade outside Europe is still quoted in US dollars.

Tip

Under conditions of international economic and political unrest, the US dollar is still considered the main safe-haven currency. It is the most actively traded currency in the world.

As a result of its imposed status as the default reserve currency under Bretton Woods, many smaller nations still use the US dollar as their official currency. This process is referred to as official dollarisation. Some countries that use the US dollar include Panama, Bermuda and the Bahamas, where the US dollar is accepted as legal tender along with the local currency at a 1:1 exchange rate. The British dependencies of the British Virgin Islands, and Turks and Caicos Islands also use the US dollar as official currency. More recently, some smaller countries, such as El Salvador in 2001 and Ecuador in 2000, have also adopted the US dollar as their official currency. When it achieved independence in 2000, Timor-Leste (East Timor) also chose the US dollar as its official currency.

Other countries link their currency to the US dollar at a fixed exchange rate, known as a linked exchange rate system. Some examples include Barbados where the local Barbados dollar is convertible to US dollars at a 2:1 ratio, and Hong Kong where the Hong Kong dollar has been linked to the US dollar since 1983 at between $7.75 and $7.85 Hong Kong dollars to the US dollar. Saudi Arabia also pegs its currency, the Saudi riyal, to the US dollar because of its role in the international oil market.

Tip

The US dollar is also accepted as a second currency in some countries although it is not officially recognised as legal tender. Examples include Peru, Uruguay and many South-East Asian countries including Vietnam, Myanmar and Cambodia. Many Canadian and Mexican businesses also accept US dollars.

The Chinese yuan and the US dollar

As China's economy continues to develop, many people are theorising on what this will mean for global markets and currency markets, particularly how it will affect the US dollar. Perhaps one of the biggest issues be if the yuan (CNY, ¥) becomes a free-floating currency and can be traded freely on forex markets, like other open market currencies. While all of this is pure speculation at present, it's handy to have some understanding of the history of the yuan and its relationship with the US dollar.

The Chinese yuan has generally been pegged to the US dollar. During the 1980s, as China's economy began to open up, the yuan was devalued on several occasions so the country could achieve export competitiveness. The official exchange rate declined from 1.50 yuan per US dollar in 1980 to 8.62 yuan per US dollar in 1994. From 1997 to July 2005 the official rate remained stable at 8.27 yuan per US dollar. On 21 July 2005 the Chinese government lifted the peg against the US dollar and replaced it with a managed floating exchange rate system based on a basket of foreign currencies representing China's major global trading partners. According to Chinese government officials, this basket of currencies is dominated by the US dollar, euro, Japanese yen and South Korean won. Other currencies included in the basket include the British pound, Russian rouble, Thai baht, Australian dollar, Canadian dollar and Singapore dollar. Under this system, the yuan is allowed to float within a narrow band of 0.5 per cent around the parity price determined by the People's Bank of China (PBC).

In July 2008, in the midst of the global financial crisis (GFC), the yuan was unofficially repegged to the US dollar. China maintains that the pegging of the yuan to the US dollar is necessary in order to protect its developing businesses and economy, and to promote economic growth. This keeps Chinese exports cheap on world markets and tips the balance of trade in China's favour. This is a source of ongoing tension with the United States, which argues that China needs to devalue the yuan to tip the trade balance more in favour of the United States. This is a political and economic debate that may continue for some time.

Tip

The Chinese government sets the value of the yuan and allows it to trade in a tight range at around 7.27 yuan to the US dollar.

The euro

The euro (EUR, €) became the official currency of the Eurozone member states of the European Union (EU) in 1999, and it is now in use in 16 of the 27 EU member states. The current Eurozone members (those countries within the EU using the euro as official currency) are Austria, Belgium, Cyprus, Finland, France, Germany, Greece, Ireland, Italy,

Luxembourg, Malta, the Netherlands, Portugal, Slovakia, Slovenia and Spain. The euro is the world's second most actively traded currency.

Within the European Union, as a prerequisite for joining the Eurozone, Bulgaria, Denmark, Estonia, Latvia and Lithuania have pegged their currency to the euro. More than twenty countries that don't belong to the EU have also pegged their currency to the euro, including many in mainland Africa. Just as the US dollar is used as a peg for smaller countries, particularly those located geographically close to the United States, many of the countries and territories using the euro as a peg for their currency are geographically close to the EU countries, or are former colonies or territories of EU member states, such as the three French Pacific territories of French Polynesia, New Caledonia, and the Territory of Wallis and Futuna Islands.

Tip

Countries with small or weaker economies often peg their currency to a major currency like the euro or US dollar. This is regarded as a safety measure, as the strength and stability of the major currency will support the local currency and economy. It may also help prevent inflation and provide peace of mind for foreign investors.

The euro is the second-largest global currency, as shown in table 2.1 (on page 26). According to the Bank of International Settlements (BIS) the euro is the second most traded currency in the world after the US dollar. According to the European Central Bank and the IMF, in October 2009 the euro surpassed the US dollar as the currency with the greatest combined value of banknotes and coins in circulation in the world, with more than €800 billion now in circulation.

After its introduction into the global foreign exchange market at US$1.18/€1 on 1 January 1999, the value of the euro fell rapidly to a low of US$0.8252/€1 in October 2000 because of concerns about its acceptance and the economic implications of one currency for the EU. In late September 2000 the European Central Bank, the Bank of England, the Bank of Japan, the Bank of Canada and the US Federal Reserve began a coordinated market intervention program aimed at halting the slide in the price of the euro. These five central banks used US$2 billion of their currency reserves to purchase euros. They cited four main reasons for intervening in the market and halting the slide in the value of the fledgling currency:

1   Rising oil prices at the time meant a declining euro would cause inflation to rise in Europe.

2   A strong US dollar and a falling euro would impact negatively on the US trade deficit and this situation was already prompting calls for more protectionism in the United States.

3   The profits of US and other multinational companies operating in Europe were being eroded.

4   The reputation of the Eurozone and the new monetary union was being damaged.

The buying intervention worked and the value of the euro began to improve, regaining parity with the US dollar in July 2002. The initial decline in value and the effects of this massive buying intervention can be seen in figure 2.1.

In May 2003 the euro surpassed the US$1.18/€1 value at its launch. Since then the euro has ebbed and flowed in line with economic and geo-political events, which has seen it become a highly liquid and highly traded currency.

Since the introduction of the euro in 1999 the importance of the US dollar as an international reserve currency has declined. Table 2.1 (overleaf) shows the currency composition of official foreign exchange reserves as reported by the IMF. The table highlights the rise in importance of the euro from around 18 per cent of reserves in 1999 to more than 27 per cent in 2009, and the fall of the US dollar from just under 71 per cent in 1999 to around 62 per cent in 2009. The US dollar is still the most commonly held reserve currency, with its holdings still standing at more than double those of the euro, although the importance of the euro is steadily rising.

Figure 2.1: price chart of the euro from launch in 1999 to October 2010

Source: Trade Navigator © Genesis Financial Technologies, Inc.

Tip

Former chairman of the US Federal Reserve Alan Greenspan said in an interview in Germany's Stern *magazine in September 2007 that the euro could replace the US dollar as the world's primary reserve currency. He said that it is 'absolutely conceivable that the euro will replace the dollar as reserve currency, or will be traded as an equally important reserve currency'.*

Table 2.1: composition of official foreign exchange reserves in percentage terms, 1995 to 2009

Currency	1995	1996	1997	1998	1999	2000	2001	2002	2003	2004	2005	2006	2007	2008	2009
US dollar	59.0	62.1	65.2	69.3	70.9	70.5	70.7	66.5	65.8	65.9	66.4	65.7	64.1	64.1	62.2
Euro	–	–	–	–	17.9	18.8	19.8	24.2	25.3	24.9	24.3	25.2	26.3	26.4	27.3
Pound sterling	2.1	2.7	2.6	2.7	2.9	2.8	2.7	2.9	2.6	3.3	3.6	4.2	4.7	4.0	4.3
Japanese yen	6.8	6.7	5.8	6.2	6.4	6.3	5.2	4.5	4.1	3.9	3.7	3.2	2.9	3.1	3.0
German mark	15.8	14.7	14.5	13.8	–	–	–	–	–	–	–	–	–	–	–
French franc	2.4	1.8	1.4	1.6	–	–	–	–	–	–	–	–	–	–	–
Swiss franc	0.3	0.2	0.4	0.3	0.2	0.3	0.3	0.4	0.2	0.2	0.1	0.2	0.2	0.1	0.1
Other	13.6	11.7	10.2	6.1	1.6	1.4	1.2	1.4	1.9	1.8	1.9	1.5	1.8	2.2	3.1

Source: IMF Currency Composition of Official Foreign Exchange Reserves.

The Japanese yen

Despite a much smaller international presence than either the US dollar or the euro, the Japanese yen (JPY, ¥) is the third most traded currency in the world. It is also widely held as a reserve currency, along with the US dollar, the euro and the British pound.

Both the Japanese economy and the value of the yen were severely damaged by World War II. Under the Bretton Woods Accord, the value of the yen was fixed at ¥360/US$1, and this exchange rate remained in place until 1971, when the Bretton Woods system began to unravel. The belief in the United States that the yen and several other currencies had become undervalued led to the actions known as the Nixon Shock, as discussed in chapter 1, and led to the devaluation of the US dollar in 1971. Japanese exports were seen as being too cheap in international markets, while imports into Japan were overpriced. Under the exchange regime proposed in the Smithsonian Agreement, the Japanese government agreed to a new fixed exchange rate of ¥308/US$1. In 1973 the Japanese yen became a free-floating currency, along with the other major world currencies.

Despite the yen becoming a free-floating currency, the Japanese government continued to intervene heavily in the foreign exchange market to maintain the yen's value against the US dollar. Most of this intervention was aimed at protecting Japan's rapidly growing industrial base from a rising yen. As an export-driven economy, Japan, and therefore the yen, is highly sensitive to rising energy costs. During the early 1980s a current account surplus in the Japanese economy generated strong trade-related demand for the yen. But high interest rates in the United States and continuing deregulation of capital markets saw a net capital outflow from Japan, which increased the supply of yen in foreign exchange markets and ensured the yen remained weak against the US dollar.

In September 1985 the Plaza Accord (so called because the meeting took place at the Plaza Hotel in New York) was agreed between Japan, France, West Germany, Britain and the United States. The five governments agreed to intervene in currency markets to depreciate the US dollar against the German mark and the Japanese yen in yet another attempt to stimulate the US economy out of recession. Between 1985 and 1987 the value of the US dollar against the yen declined by more than 50 per cent as the central banks of the signatories to the Plaza Accord spent an estimated US$10 billion in the currency markets. The effect on the value of the US dollar against the yen is shown in figure 2.2.

Figure 2.2: effect of the Plaza Accord, 1978 to 2003

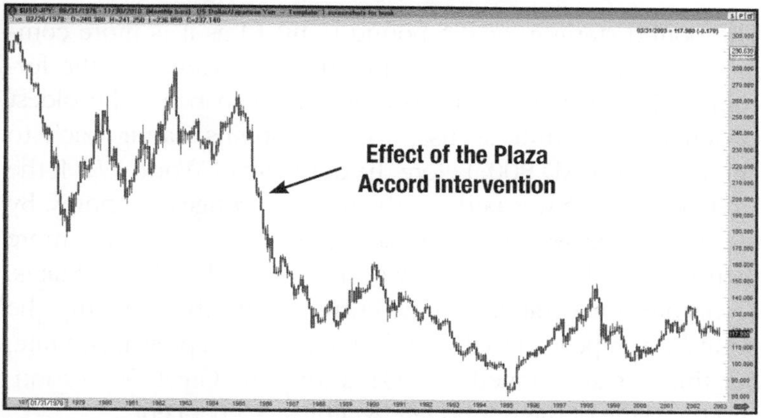

Effect of the Plaza
Accord intervention

Source: Trade Navigator © Genesis Financial Technologies, Inc.

The idea behind devaluing the US dollar was to make US exports to its major trading partners in Europe and Japan cheaper, thus encouraging these countries to buy more US-made goods. The Plaza Accord achieved this with the US's European trading partners, but failed in alleviating the trade deficit with Japan. This has been attributed to Japan's somewhat protectionist import restrictions. The strengthened yen led to an asset and housing price bubble, and a serious recession in Japan during the 1990s. Many economists and analysts refer to this period as the lost decade — a period from which the yen has still not fully recovered.

From a forex trading perspective the yen is a highly liquid currency that is traded in a number of the major currency crosses including against the US dollar, the euro, the British pound and the Australian dollar. This is discussed in detail in chapter 5.

The yen is seen as a safe-haven currency in times of economic turmoil and geo-political unrest. It is also used as an interest rate carry trade currency, because of the very low interest rates in Japan. The carry trade will be discussed in more detail in chapter 6.

The British pound

The pound sterling, or the pound (GBP, £) as it is more commonly known, is the fourth most traded currency in the foreign exchange markets. It also lays claim to being the oldest currency in continuous use, with its origins dating back to before the year AD 800. Before the outbreak of World War I, the United Kingdom was perhaps the world's strongest economy. By the end of the war it is estimated that the country was more than £850 million in debt, owed mostly to the United States. To restore some stability to the currency and the economy, the pound was repegged to the gold standard at the prewar peg rate, but this was abandoned in 1931 during the Great Depression, and the value of the pound fell by almost 25 per cent.

During World War II the pound was pegged to the US dollar at £1/US$4.03, and this rate remained in place under the Bretton Woods Accord, until the British government, in response to pressure that the pound was significantly overvalued, devalued the pound by 30 per cent in September 1949 to a value of £1/US$2.80 Like all the other major currencies, the British pound became a free-floating currency in 1973. The pound had a wild ride during the 1980s, initially rising in line with rising interest rates, crashing heavily in the middle of the decade during the deep recession that followed, and then rising again towards the end of 1989 as the economy slowly recovered. In October 1990, Britain joined the European exchange rate mechanism (ERM) to ensure the pound would not fluctuate by more than 6 per cent against the value of other EU member currencies.

The ERM was introduced by the European Community as part of the European monetary system (EMS) to achieve monetary stability and in preparation for the introduction of the euro currency. The ERM is essentially a semi-pegged exchange rate system that allows fixed currency exchange rates to fluctuate within a tight band; it is used as part of the processes for evaluating potential Eurozone member states.

Black Wednesday

With Britain having joined the ERM, the pound was set at a value of £1 to 2.95 German marks (£1/DM2.95). Under the terms of the ERM it was to be allowed to fluctuate by 6 per cent either side of this value. The lower limit for the pound (the point at which the government had to intervene to support the pound) was set at DM2.77. With interest rates higher in Germany and Europe in general than in Britain, the British economy being battered by a depreciating US dollar, and high and ever-increasing inflation, there was considerable pressure from all quarters for Britain to increase its interest rate in line with the other European economies and devalue its currency.

Financier George Soros's hedge funds began short selling British pounds, believing that current exchange rates were unsustainable and would have to fall or be devalued. On 16 September 1992, what is now known as Black Wednesday, events came to a head. The British government lifted interest rates to 15 per cent in an attempt to prevent the pound falling further, and it withdrew from the ERM. But the selling of the pound continued. Soros's fund had short sold US$10 billion worth of pounds, and it is estimated that the profit from these trades was around US$1 billion. Soros became known in financial circles as the man who 'broke' the Bank of England.

The wild journey of the British pound and the effects of Black Wednesday are shown in figure 2.3.

Figure 2.3: the value of the British pound in the 1980s and the effects of Black Wednesday in 1992

Source: Trade Navigator © Genesis Financial Technologies, Inc.

As a member of the European Union, Britain could use the euro as its currency, but the government continues to procrastinate over the issue. Debate continues on the subject and remains controversial with the British public, the majority of whom continue to support the use of the pound. In addition, it is doubtful whether the criteria required to meet the use of the euro as defined under the Maastricht Treaty could be met by Britain. For example, the current government deficit as a percentage of GDP is above the threshold required by the EU.

Tip

The pound and the euro trade independently of each other, and fluctuate against each other according to variations in interest rates and economic conditions between Britain and Eurozone members. There does, however, appear to be a high degree of correlation between the movements in the exchange rates of the two currencies when compared with those of other major currencies, particularly the US dollar.

The Australian dollar

The Aussie dollar (AUD, $) is currently the fifth most traded currency. The general stability of the Australian economy and political system has contributed to the increased interest in the Australian dollar. Other factors that encourage trading in the Australian dollar include the country's geographical location and export business with Asian countries, relatively high interest rates, its exposure to the commodity cycle, and government's the general lack of intervention in the exchange rate mechanism.

Tip

The Aussie dollar is considered a commodity-based currency because of the country's reliance on the export of minerals, including gold, and other raw materials.

As Australia was a British colony, its original currency was the British pound. This was replaced by the Australian pound in 1910, which was in turn replaced by the Australian dollar in 1966, when the exchange rate was pegged to the British pound at AUD2.50/GBP1, reflecting the country's historical and economic ties with Britain. In 1967 the Australian dollar was pegged to the US dollar at AUD1/USD1.12. In 1971, following the breakdown of the Bretton Woods Accord, Australia pegged its currency to a fluctuating rate against the US dollar. In 1974, in line with continued concerns regarding the US economy and a desire to reduce the fluctuations associated with the floating peg to the US dollar, Australia began valuing the dollar against a basket of currencies called the trade weighted index (TWI). At any one time there were up to 22 currencies within the TWI, the weight of each being dependent on trade values between Australia and each country. This system remained in place until December 1983, when deregulation of the Australian financial system saw the Aussie dollar become a free-floating currency along with the other major world currencies, with its value determined by supply and demand factors instead of government policy and intervention.

Since becoming a free-floating currency, the Aussie dollar has ranged from a low of AUD1/USD0.47 in April 2001 to a high of just over parity in November 2010.

The Australian dollar has a unique and interesting place in the global foreign exchange market. Because Australia's balance of trade is highly dependent on commodity exports, including minerals and agricultural products, the value of the Australian dollar tends to be inverse to those of the other major currencies. During global booms, when raw materials are needed for manufacturing and increased consumption, the Aussie dollar tends to rally. When mineral prices slump or demand for commodities slows down, the Aussie dollar declines in value.

Tip

During times of economic uncertainty the Aussie dollar loses its appeal, and traders and investors move back into the so-called safe-haven currencies, including the US dollar, the yen and the euro.

Increasing globalisation and deregulation means the Aussie dollar is also influenced by interest rate differentials, rising and falling global share prices, and international geo-political concerns and events. As a result, the Australian dollar tends to display a fairly high degree of volatility. This volatility and its unique and unorthodox place in the global financial system have been major factors in contributing to its status as one of the world's most actively traded currencies.

One of the major influences on the Australian dollar in recent times has been the strengthening commodity market cycle and the huge demand for resources from China. This has had a positive impact on the value of the Australian dollar, as its resources-driven export cycle has continued to flourish even as the United States and Europe have suffered from the after-effects of the global financial crisis. Asian economies, particularly China's, have been growing strongly and the demand for Australia's commodity resources continues to be high.

The Swiss franc

The origins of the Swiss franc (CHF, Fr) can be traced back to before 1798. It is currently the sixth most traded currency in the world. In the early 1800s an estimated 8000 different types of notes and coins were in circulation in Switzerland. In 1848, the new Swiss federal constitution, which united the various cantons or states after a short civil war, specified that only the newly formed federal government could print money, thereby stabilising and centralising the banking system. In May 1850 the Swiss franc was introduced as the sole currency unit for Switzerland.

Along with France, Belgium and Italy, Switzerland formed the Latin Monetary Union in 1865, agreeing to value their currencies at a standard of either 4.5 grams of silver or 0.29 grams of gold. This monetary union ended in 1927, but the Swiss maintained the same valuation standard until 1936. Following devaluations of the British pound, French franc and US dollar in September 1936, the Swiss franc experienced its one and only devaluation. Under the Bretton Woods system the Swiss franc was pegged at 4.30521CHF/US$1, or the equivalent of 0.206418 grams of gold.

Historically the Swiss franc has been considered a safe-haven currency. Much of this idea is attributed to a history within the Swiss economy of zero inflation and the requirement that a minimum of 40 per cent of the currency in circulation be backed by gold reserves, creating a pseudo-gold standard, and the strength and quality of the Swiss financial system. The gold cover enabled the Swiss franc to remain relatively stable and also greatly contributed to the attractiveness of the Swiss banking system to international investors.

Tip

Following a referendum in May 2000, the gold cover of the Swiss franc was reduced to 20 per cent, perhaps reducing some of the appeal of the Swiss franc as a safe-haven currency. Nonetheless, the appeal of the Swiss franc during uncertain economic times, and periods of economic and political upheaval and unrest, remains due to the gold reserves that still back the Swiss franc.

The Canadian dollar

The Canadian dollar (CAD, $) is currently the seventh most traded currency on global foreign exchange markets. As a former colony of Britain, like Australia, Canada used the British pound as its currency from 1764 until around 1841, when the Canadian pound was adopted by some areas of Canada. Years of debate followed, with the majority of Canadians wishing to adopt a decimal currency system based on the US dollar, while boffins in London wanted to maintain use of the British pound throughout the British Empire. In 1853, the gold standard was introduced, based on both British gold sovereigns and American gold coins at a rate of £1/US$4.8666 with both currencies being used in various Canadian provinces or states. In 1858 decimal coinage was introduced and Canada's currency became aligned with the US dollar. In 1871, the Canadian parliament passed the Uniform Currency Act, replacing the currencies of the provinces and the Canadian pound with the Canadian dollar, which was linked to the gold standard.

Having abandoned the gold standard in 1933, the Canadian dollar was pegged at CAD$1.1/US$1 during World War II. This was changed to parity in 1946. Then, following a devaluation in 1949, the value returned to the original peg value of CAD$1.1/$US1. Unlike other currencies in the Bretton Woods system, whose values were pegged to the US dollar, the Canadian dollar was allowed to float from 1950 to 1962. The Canadian dollar returned to a fixed exchange rate in 1962, when its value was set at CAD$1/US$0.925, which remained in force until 1970, when the Canadian dollar once again became a free-floating currency.

Like the Australian dollar, the Canadian dollar is considered a commodity-based currency, mainly because of Canada's position as a major oil exporter. As such, the Canadian dollar plays a similar role in the northern hemisphere to that which the Australian dollar plays in the Asia–Pacific region—providing exposure to a resource-based economy and currency, and being held as a reserve currency as a result.

Tip

Movements in the Canadian dollar exchange rate tend to be correlated to the price of crude oil and energy prices, rising and falling in line with movements in the price of these energy commodities. It is often referred to as a petrocurrency because of this close correlation.

Because of the country's close proximity to the United States, and its reliance on the US for more than 80 per cent of its exports and more than 50 per cent of its imports, Canadians have a close interest in the value of the US dollar, as the relative values have a direct economic effect on Canada's economy. The Bank of Canada maintains an official position that market conditions should determine the value of the

Canadian dollar, and it claims to have not directly intervened in foreign exchange markets since 1988. Table 2.2 shows the world's most traded currencies.

Table 2.2: currency distribution of global foreign exchange as a percentage of market turnover, selected years 1998 to 2001

Currency	1998	2001	2004	2007	2010
US dollar	86.8	89.9	88	85.6	84.9
Euro	N/a	37.9	37.4	37	39.1
Japanese yen	21.7	23.5	20.8	17.2	19.0
British pound	11.0	13	16.5	14.9	12.9
Australian dollar	3.0	4.3	6.0	6.6	7.6
Swiss franc	7.1	6.0	6.0	6.8	6.4
Canadian dollar	3.5	4.5	4.2	4.3	5.3
Other	66.9	20.9	21.1	27.6	24.8

Source: Bank of International Settlements Triennial Central Bank Survey, April 2010.
Note: The total of each column adds up to 200 per cent, as currencies are always traded in pairs—one against the other (for more information, see chapter 5).

Central banks

A country's central or reserve bank is the financial institution that oversees the operation of the country's banking and monetary system. A central bank will usually have several areas of responsibility, including:

⇨ issuing the national currency

⇨ regulating the money supply

⇨ implementing monetary policy and controlling interest rates

⇨ controlling inflation and price stability

⇨ maintaining currency values

⇨ ensuring stability of the financial system including regulating and supervising the commercial banks

⇨ acting as lender of last resort to commercial banks

⇨ acting as the government's banker

⇨ managing foreign exchange reserves.

An independent central bank will ensure there is no political influence over the central bank's policies and that the policies of the central bank will be neutral in regard to the governing political regime. This is particularly important during times of rising inflation or rising interest rates, which are politically sensitive issues.

Tip

As foreign exchange traders, we are most interested in the role of the central banks in using monetary policy to achieve a central bank's objectives in terms of controlling inflation and unemployment levels; its intervention in the financial securities markets to attempt to control and manipulate interest rates and the money supply (often referred to as open market operations); and its management of foreign exchange reserve levels, and the impact these actions have on currency values.

Monetary policy

Monetary policy is the management of money supply to achieve the goals of stable prices, low unemployment, low inflation and sustainable levels of economic growth. Monetary policy is handled by a country's central bank, and is in sharp contrast to fiscal policy, which refers to government spending, borrowing and taxation. The monetary policy tools available to a central bank to achieve these objectives and to influence the level of economic activity include:

⇨ interest rates

⇨ open market operations

⇨ reserve requirements.

All three have the effect of either expanding or contracting the money supply within an economy. Monetary policy is referred to as being either expansionary or contractionary. Expansionary monetary policy rapidly increases the supply of money in the economy and is used to encourage employment and economic growth by lowering interest rates. Contractionary policy is used to control rising inflation or combat inflationary pressures by decreasing, or slowly increasing, the money supply by raising interest rates.

Tip

Monetary policies exist and can be implemented by central banks because all the reserve currencies are fiat money. Fiat money has no intrinsic value, as it is not legally convertible to anything, nor is it fixed to any standard value. It can be created from nothing at any time by the simple act of printing more money.

Interest rates

Influencing market interest rates is perhaps the most visible of the monetary policy tools available to a central bank. Raising interest rates impacts directly on households through its effect on mortgage payments, and interest payments on other loans and consumer debt. This in turn serves to reduce consumer spending, because less money is then available to consumers. Higher interest rates also discourage new borrowing, which decreases the amount of new money created through loans. Raising interest rates is a contractionary policy designed to slow down spending and the economy, and to reduce inflationary pressures. Conversely, a cut in interest rates means more money is available for consumer spending, which encourages more borrowing and has an expansionary effect and a positive impact on economic growth.

Tip

The effect of changing interest rates on the currency markets is generally an increase in the value of a currency in line with interest rate rises, and a decrease in the value of a currency when interest rates are cut.

A contributing factor to the strength of the Australian dollar since the global financial crisis has been the relatively high level of interest rates in Australia compared with those available in the rest of the world. Higher interest rates lead to an increase in the demand for the currency by investors and speculators. It is also an important component of the carry trade, which is discussed in detail in chapter 6.

Open market operations

Open market operations involve the central bank buying and selling government securities (mainly bonds) in the open market. This is a policy measure used to control the amount of money circulating in a country's economy. When a central bank buys government securities, the effect is to expand the money supply and reduce interest rates. When a central bank sells bonds, its action takes money out of the economy, so the money supply is reduced and interest rates rise. The effect on the currency is similar to that of direct interest rate changes where, generally speaking, lower rates lead to a fall in the currency, and higher interest rates will cause the value of the currency to rise.

For the central bank to buy government securities or foreign currency in the open market, it needs new money to be available to pay for its purchases, which requires the bank to print or create this new money. This is only possible because of the fiat money system under which the global economy now operates.

As most transactions are conducted electronically and money is held as electronic records, these open market operations are conducted by electronically debiting or crediting accounts, rather than the printing or destruction of actual cash money.

If the central bank is buying in the open market, the seller's account is credited electronically, thus increasing the amount of money in that account and in the economy through the creation of new money. If the central bank is selling in the open market, the buyer's account is debited electronically, which decreases the amount of money in the account, effectively destroying that money by removing it from circulation within the economy.

Reserve requirements

In many countries the commercial banks and other financial institutions that hold customer cash deposits are required to hold a percentage of these deposits and account balances on deposit at the central bank. This is known as the reserve requirement or cash reserve ratio. In the Eurozone, for example, this reserve requirement is currently 2 per cent. This percentage amount generally remains stable and is seldom varied, though it can be used by the central bank to affect the money supply. If the reserve requirement percentage is increased, the supply of money in the economy is reduced, and interest rates will rise in response to less money being available. A rise in interest rates will generally result in an increase in the value of the country's currency. Altering reserve requirements causes a major long-term shift in the money supply, and so this method of influencing the economy is rarely used.

Central banks and the foreign exchange market

It's useful for foreign exchange traders to have some insight into the operations of central banks in the foreign exchange markets. While this knowledge may not have a direct impact on your trading, it will certainly help you understand how the actions of the central banks can affect and move the markets.

Repurchase agreements

Repurchase agreements (also known as repos or sale and purchase agreements) are transactions in government securities. The purchase of a security comes with an agreement by the seller to buy it back at a specified future date and at a price greater than the sale price. The difference is effectively an interest payment, and it is referred to as the repo rate. As the seller of the repo is effectively a borrower, and the buyer is a lender, a repo is a cash transaction combined with a forward contract. Forward contracts are explained in chapter 3. When transacted by a central bank, the purchase of repos adds temporary or short-term reserves to the banking system; and then the reserves are withdrawn when the repo is recalled.

Tip

The purchase of repos by the country's central bank generally results in a reduction in the value of the currency on foreign exchange markets.

A reverse repo, or matched sale, occurs when the central bank sells repos. The result is a temporary draining of funds from the banking system, which pushes up interest rates, and increases the price of the currency on foreign exchange markets.

Foreign exchange intervention

Intervention in the foreign exchange markets by central banks and government treasury departments is a sensitive issue. It is aimed at achieving and maintaining orderly market conditions, though the definition of what constitutes orderly will depend on the economic goals of individual countries and the relative strength or weakness of individual currencies. For that reason, any direct intervention is typically conducted with a degree of stealth and secrecy, and the action is generally not announced to the market, though there are examples of central banks openly collaborating to influence currency values, such as after the Plaza Accord and the intervention buying of the Euro as discussed above.

Naked, or unsterilised, intervention is the direct buying or selling of a country's currency by its central bank. Naked intervention leads to changes in the money supply, and can add to inflationary and other pressures within an economy. Sterilised intervention, by comparison, involves offsetting the impact of intervention in the currency markets on other areas of the economy selling or buying government securities to offset the money either generated through the sale of the currency, or the money spent buying the currency.

Tip

Sterilised intervention is generally the preferred option for most central banks, as it is has less direct impact on the underlying economy. It is generally used as a short-term to medium-term measure.

The rise of central banks

Central banks came to prominence following the collapse of the gold standard. Before that, currencies were generally backed by gold or silver, which meant price stability was easy to maintain. Monetary expansion was then only possible if the amount of gold held by a country also increased. Regardless of the creditworthiness of a government, the value of its currency was supported by the value of the underlying precious metal, and countries held stores of gold and silver in order to support the value of the currency. With the advent of paper money, and the potential to simply produce more money with a printing press and some ink, it too was backed by a 'promise to pay', which led to the introduction of the gold standard.

Following the Great Depression of the 1930s, economist John Maynard Keynes introduced the concept of monetary policy to influence the supply of money in an economy and thus provide ways of influencing economic activity. Again, this system is only possible with fiat currencies that are not backed by anything of value and have no intrinsic value.

Tip

The issuance of currency must also be controlled by a monopoly monetary authority to ensure money is not simply created on an ad-hoc basis.

Since the 1930s, it has become the role of the central banks to control the amount of money and credit available in an economy, and to achieve other economic requirements through monetary policy as discussed above. A major role of a central bank operating a fiat money system is to maintain the purchasing power of a currency and its worth compared with other currencies—this is a complex task, as most countries now have open economies that allow the free movement of capital, and free of currency movements on the global foreign exchange markets.

The most important central banks are:

⇨ US Federal Reserve System

⇨ European Central Bank

⇨ Bank of Japan

⇨ Bank of England

⇨ Reserve Bank of Australia

⇨ Swiss National Bank

⇨ Bank of Canada.

US Federal Reserve System

Created in 1913 under the Federal Reserve Act, the mandate of the US Federal Reserve System (also known as the Fed) includes maintaining the stability of the country's financial system, conducting monetary policy, and achieving price stability and long-term economic growth for US citizens. It comprises a chairperson and board of governors appointed by the US president, the presidents of 12 regional Federal Reserve Banks and representatives from other private US member banks. The Federal Open Market Committee (FOMC) is the group within the Fed that makes interest rate decisions.

Tip

The US Federal Reserve System is still the most influential central bank in the world, and decisions made by the Federal Reserve Board have a significant impact on global financial markets.

The makeup of the US Federal Reserve System is unique among central banks because it is partly a public and partly a privately run institution and, unlike other central banks, it is not directly responsible for the creation of the US currency. This often gives rise to debate as to just how independent the Fed is, and to whom it owes its strongest allegiances—the American people, or the banking system.

European Central Bank

Established in 1998 by the Treaty of Amsterdam, the European Central Bank (ECB) administers the monetary policy of the 16 Eurozone member states. The mandate of the ECB is price stability, long-term economic growth and an annual inflation target of less than 2 per cent. Other key areas of activity include conducting foreign exchange operations to manage the foreign exchange reserves of the national banks of the EU member states, and monitoring and maintaining the Eurozone banking sector.

The Governing Council is the main decision-making body of the ECB. It comprises the six members of the Executive Board, and the governors of the national banks of the 16 Eurozone members. The ECB is an independent organisation within the EU, effectively managing the monetary policy for member states. It is known to provide markets with ample warning of any impending policy changes.

Bank of Japan

The Bank of Japan (BoJ) has operated continuously since its establishment in 1882, though it has had a number of policy revisions and reorganisations over the years. Its current mandate includes currency and monetary control, price stability and the development of the national economy. Because Japan has an export-driven economy, the Bank of Japan has an interest in preventing a strong Japanese yen, because a high-value currency has a negative effect on Japan's export businesses. The Bank of Japan has been known to directly intervene in the currency market to weaken the yen by selling it against the US dollar and the euro when it is concerned about the relative value of the yen.

The Policy Board, which includes the governor, two deputy governors, and six other board members, is responsible for all major policy decisions. Although cooperation with the government is expected, the Bank of Japan operates as an independent central bank. Government officials can attend board meetings, but only in a non-voting capacity.

Bank of England

The origins of the Bank of England (BoE) can be traced back to 1694, though its role has changed over the last 300 years. It is the central bank for the whole United Kingdom and is the model upon which most modern central banks are based. It was privately owned and operated until it was nationalised in 1946, and became an independent public organisation in 1997, when it was given statutory authority for setting the interest rates in the United Kingdom. Its two core purposes are monetary stability and financial stability, and it maintains an inflation target of 2 per cent per year, similar to that of the ECB.

The Bank of England is managed by a court of directors, all of whom are appointed by the government, and which includes a governor, two deputy governors and nine non-executive directors. It has a nine-member monetary policy committee consisting of the governor, two deputy governors, two executive directors and four external advisers.

The Bank of England had a difficult period during the 1990s when, despite double digit inflation, Britain agreed to join the EU's exchange rate mechanism. The BoE was able to keep the British pound within the 6 per cent range allowed under the ERM for a short period. Eventually, however, the pressure of the artificially high interest rates required to maintain the pound's value against the German mark and a weak domestic economy, combined with a huge speculative short sale by George Soros's hedge fund, created the events of Black Wednesday in September 1992.

Reserve Bank of Australia

The *Reserve Bank Act 1959* established the Reserve Bank of Australia (RBA) as the Australia's central bank. Like all the major central banks, the RBA carries out open market operations, transactions in foreign exchange markets, and monetary policy operations in order to meet its mandate of a stable currency, the maintenance of full employment, and economic prosperity and welfare in a low-inflation environment of between 2 and 3 per cent.

The RBA has two boards: the Reserve Bank Board, which is responsible for monetary policy and financial stability, and the Payments System Board, which is responsible for the credit and payment systems. The Reserve Bank Board has nine members: the governor, who is appointed by the federal government treasurer, a deputy governor, the secretary to the treasurer, and six non-executive external members, who are also appointed by the government. Members of the RBA board must not be a director, officer or employee of any authorised depository institution.

Tip

The complex nature of the Australian economy in the commodity cycle, the inverse relationship of the Australian dollar to the other major currencies, and the boom and bust nature of the Australian economy provide continuing challenges for the RBA. It often struggles to get monetary policy timing decisions to line up with what is really happening in the economy.

Swiss National Bank

The central bank of the Swiss Confederation, the Swiss National Bank (SNB) commenced operations in 1907. It is an independent central bank with the primary goals of price stability (an inflation rate of 2 per cent per annum or less) and economic growth in the best interests of the country.

The SNB has a two-tiered governing structure—an 11-member Governing Council, with six government-appointed members and five elected members, and a three-member Governing Board comprising the chairperson, vice chairperson, and one other member, all appointed by the government. The Governing Board has complete responsibility for monetary policy and overall strategic planning.

The Swiss National Bank uses open market operations and facilities to influence interest rates and to implement its monetary policy. Unlike other central banks it sets a target range for a reference interest rate rather than a specific defined rate. It also relies entirely on open market operations to manage the value of the Swiss franc on currency markets. As well as the use of open market repo transactions to affect currency liquidity, the SNB also mandates the amount of currency that commercial banks must hold as reserves. These must be held as Swiss franc banknotes, coins, or sight deposits (funds that can be transferred between various accounts and can be quickly converted to cash) held at the SNB. This reserve requirement is currently set at 2.5 per cent, but can be increased to a maximum of 4 per cent if necessary. The SNB also manages the official gold reserves, which are used to back the currency.

Bank of Canada

Created by the Bank of Canada Act of 1934, the Bank of Canada's principal role is the economic and financial welfare of the Canadian people. Like all central banks, its mandate includes ensuring low and stable inflation, financial security and currency management. It has a specific aim to keep inflation maintained at between 1 and 3 per cent.

The Governing Council is responsible for all monetary policy decisions. This council comprises the governor of the Bank of Canada, the senior deputy governor, and four deputy governors, who are appointed by the bank's board of directors. The deputy minister of finance sits on the board but does not have a vote.

Tip

The Bank of Canada favours the use of interest rates as its inflationary control mechanism. Since 1998 the bank has maintained a policy of not intervening in the foreign exchange market, except under exceptional circumstances, preferring instead that the value of the Canadian dollar be determined by supply and demand for the currency.

Chapter summary

⇨ Although all countries have their own currency, foreign exchange trading is limited to the currencies that have a global presence through their use in international trade and investment.

⇨ The United States dollar (USD, $) effectively became the world's reserve currency under the Bretton Woods Accord. As a result the US dollar remains the world's main currency with most global trade outside of Europe still being quoted in US dollars.

⇨ Of major interest in the future will be whether the Chinese yuan becomes a free-floating currency and can be freely traded on forex markets like other open market currencies.

⇨ Since the introduction of the euro in 1999, the importance of the US dollar as an international reserve currency has declined. The US dollar is still the most-held reserve currency, with holdings still more than double that of the euro, but the importance of the euro is steadily increasing.

⇨ Despite a much smaller international presence than either the US dollar or the euro, the Japanese yen is the third most traded currency in the world.

⇨ The British pound was subject to one of the most aggressive attacks on the value of a currency in September 1992 by a large hedge fund, which was convinced that the pound was over-valued.

⇨ Both the Australian dollar and Canadian dollar are referred to as commodity currencies because of the reliance of these two economies on raw materials.

⇨ The Swiss franc is still backed by a 20 per cent gold reserve.

⇨ A central or reserve bank is the financial institution that oversees the operation of the banking and monetary system within a country.

⇨ Monetary policy is the main tool central banks use to control interest rates and currency values.

⇨ The mandate of all the central banks is very similar, with a focus on low inflation, currency stability, economic growth and prosperity within an economy.

chapter 3

The foreign exchange markets and major participants

Now that we have an insight into the major currencies and their economies, and the important role that central banks play within an economy and the foreign exchange, or forex, markets, we now need to deepen our understanding of the forex market before we begin forex trading.

We need to understand who the major players in these markets are and the types of forex markets available.

Forex market participants

As well as the central banks and their role in and influence on the global foreign exchange market, many other participants are involved in the trading of foreign exchange. It is important to know who these other players are, where they fit in the market and the roles they play within the foreign exchange market.

Tip

The foreign exchange, or forex, market is divided into levels of access that are determined by the size of the line, or amount of money, being traded in each transaction.

The inter-bank market

After the central banks, the large global commercial banks and financial institutions are the major participants in the forex market, and together they form the inter-bank market. While central bank operations in the market may be sporadic, the large commercial banks are actively involved in foreign exchange trading every day. Their trading activities add massive liquidity and volume to the market daily and are the main cause of price movement in the markets. Major international banks deal either directly with each other or through two main electronic platforms, EBS and Reuters, which offer trading in the major currency pairs. The banks regularly undertake trades worth billions of dollars on behalf of clients or, more commonly, speculateing on their own accounts. They are responsible for the majority of forex trading volume.

The inter-bank market is an unregulated and decentralised wholesale market that works around the world and around the clock. These banks effectively act as market makers in the spot forex market (discussed later in this chapter), as they are constantly quoting buy and sell prices in anticipation of movements in currency prices.

Tip

The forex price quotes we see on our trading platforms are the result of the transactions between the large banks and financial institutions in the inter-bank market. Their activity tends to set the buy and sell quotes that are then made available to retail brokers and traders.

Companies and businesses

Multinational companies are often participants in the forex markets, conducting transactions related to the purchase or sale of goods and raw materials, or the conversion of overseas earnings into the company's domestic currency. Much of their activity involves hedging against adverse currency movements to protect their overseas and import and export operations, or to lock in favourable exchange rates. However, many also speculate in the currency markets. The activities of these large companies add further liquidity and volatility to the forex markets. They often have larger positions, unknown to other market participants, which they implement or cover quickly and unexpectedly, resulting in sharp and sudden price moves.

Hedge funds

Large hedge funds that trade in all markets for speculative purposes to generate above average returns for their investors are also participants in the foreign exchange market. They speculate aggressively and can take large positions by using the leverage offered in the forex markets. (Leverage is explained in detail in chapter 5.) Perhaps the most famous example of hedge fund involvement in the currency markets is the 1992 attack on the British pound by George Soros's hedge fund as discussed in chapter 2. Most hedge funds, however, tend to be trend followers, building into positions over time and capturing large price movements.

Tip

Hedge funds are unregulated private investment companies that use high-risk strategies to dramatically increase returns to the investors involved.

As price speculators, hedge funds are interested only in profiting from price movements in currencies either by being long in a market trending upwards or short in a down-trending market.

Investment management firms

These firms manage large accounts on behalf of pension and superannuation funds, and they often have international share portfolios and other international investments. They use the currency markets to buy and sell currencies in line with their international investment transactions and to hedge currency risks associated with their international share and property holdings. They are not involved in the currency markets for speculative purposes.

Retail foreign exchange brokers and traders

The development of the internet and the advent of online trading platforms has revolutionised trading for retail and private traders across all markets. In the forex market the large banks were not set up to service the needs of retail players trading with small amounts of capital but who still wanted to take advantage of the opportunities offered by trading the currency markets. This initially led to the formation of the International Money Market (IMM) for the trading of currency futures, and then to the use of the spot forex market by retail traders through online broking companies that can provide access to the inter-bank market for smaller retail clients. The high liquidity and 24-hour availability of the forex market make it particularly appealing to speculators wanting to achieve a return on their capital by buying and selling currencies.

Retail and small traders provide liquidity and price discovery (the determination of price through the interaction of buyers and sellers) to the market, making it easier for hedgers and other market participants to offset their risk. Retail and small traders are the largest section by number within the overall forex market, executing millions of independent trades every day. Although the value of these trades is small compared with the trading activities of the commercial banks and other large traders, we represent a growing and important component of the currency markets.

Tip

As risk seekers seeking to make profits from their buying and selling activities, speculators play an important role within any market place.

Various currency markets

Trading currencies is conducted in one of three ways, through:

1   forwards and swaps market

2   currency futures

3   spot forex or retail forex market.

While most of the hype in the forex space is concerned with the spot forex market, currency futures contracts are also a highly liquid and tradeable product that should be considered as a viable trading vehicle. The vast majority of retail forex traders will never use forwards or swaps, but some readers of this book involved in international business transactions may use them. It is important to understand what they are and how they are used to build a deeper understanding of the role they play in forex pricing and liquidity. Let's take a look at each of these forex products and where they fit in the overall forex market, and how they add significant volume and liquidity to the foreign exchange markets. A whole book could be written about each of these products and the intricate workings and inter relationships between them. What follows is an introduction to, and brief overview of, each.

The forwards and swap market

This market consists of two main instruments—forward deals and swaps.

Tip

The forward currency market is used mostly by large institutions and companies for both hedging and speculating.

Forward outrights or currency forward contracts

Referred to simply as *forwards*, these consist of a non-standardised contract between two parties to buy or sell a specified amount of a currency at an agreed exchange rate (called the delivery price) at an agreed future date. These forward dates are normally between two days and 24 months from the current date. The terms of the contract are agreed directly between the two parties involved and the trade does not take place on a regulated exchange. As a result, any currency can be used, provided both parties agree on the terms and conditions of the transaction.

The price of the forward is based on the existing exchange rate on the spot market at the time the deal is agreed, plus an adjustment factor, which represents the interest rate differential between the two currencies. These are known as the forward points, and they can be set either at a discount or a premium to the current spot rate, depending on what the parties involved believe interest rates and thus currency exchange rates will do between the current date and the date on which the forward matures. The forward outright rate is determined by adjusting the current spot rate by the discount or premium points.

The party agreeing to buy the currency assumes a long position, and the party agreeing to sell the currency assumes a short position. A forward may have a specified maturity date or it may mature within a specified date window. This window is a specified period within which the contract can be exercised by the buyer, and it may vary from a week to one month, depending on the terms agreed by the two parties.

Tip

Forward outrights can be used for speculating on interest rate and currency movements, but they are generally used to hedge foreign exchange exposure risks or to stabilise future cash flows based on the current exchange rate.

Trading in forward outrights for speculative purposes is a complex operation that aims to take advantage of interest rate differentials between two currencies, with the trader effectively speculating on movements in four different rates. When trading the Australian dollar/US dollar (AUD/USD) as a forward outright, for example, the four variables that can determine if the trader makes a profit or a loss are changes in Australian interest rates, changes in US interest rates, movements in the AUD/USD spot rate, and changes in the AUD/USD forward rate.

Forwards are more commonly used by those seeking to hedge the value of a currency. Companies trading internationally can experience volatility in their foreign exchange exposure that can increase risk and uncertainty in the expected profit. Forwards allow companies to lock in foreign currency transactions for a future date at a rate agreed to now. The net effect is to neutralise any exchange rate fluctuations.

An importer may, for example, have ordered goods from a supplier in the United States. They make one payment when the goods are ordered, with a second payment due in four months' time when the goods are dispatched. The first payment is made immediately at the prevailing exchange rate of 0.9850 AUD/USD, and the importer wants to lock in this exchange rate for the second payment. The current or spot rate has to be adjusted for the forward points for the four-month period to the second payment. This figure is agreed at a premium of 0.0045, making the forward rate 0.9895 (the spot rate of 0.9850 plus the 0.0045 forward points = 0.9895). The importer now knows the exact exchange rate they will pay in four months' time and it is not exposed to any adverse exchange rate movements. They have hedged their exposure and risk. The downside is, of course, that they have given up the potential to profit from any favourable exchange rate movements.

Forwards are also used by international portfolio managers in much the same way, allowing them to lock in exchange rates for international deals. Commercial banks also use forwards for liquidity and risk management, and for speculative purposes.

Forward outrights are negotiated over the counter (OTC) between the parties involved. As a result they are non-standardised in terms of their contract size, settlement date and price, providing a high degree of flexibility for users of these products. One of the major downsides is that both parties involved in the transaction are exposed to the credit risk associated with the possibility that either party may default on the deal.

Non-deliverable forwards

A non-deliverable forward (NDF) is a short-term, cash-settled currency transaction between two counterparties. An

NDF is similar to a forward outright, except that no physical delivery of the principal or notional amount takes place. On the contract settlement date only the difference between the forward agreed rate and the prevailing spot rate is exchanged as either a profit or a loss in cash. Because NDFs are non-cash, off-balance sheet transactions where the principal sums do not actually change hands, they offer much lower counterparty risk than forward outrights.

NDFs are typically quoted and settled in US dollars. All NDFs have a fixing date, which is the date the agreement is made and the exchange rate calculated, and a settlement date, which is the due date for the payment of the cash difference.

The NDF market has evolved as a result of restrictions in some countries on currency exchange movements. NDFs allow the hedging of currencies that could not otherwise be hedged because of these restrictions. NDFs are used by companies seeking to hedge their exposure to non-convertible foreign currency, such as the Korean won and other emerging market currencies, where the companies' business activities create foreign exchange exposure.

Tip

NDFs are also used by banks and other large speculators seeking to profit from moves in the interest rates and exchange rates of currencies where a spot market is unavailable, and where expected or anticipated regulatory changes will affect the exchange rate.

NDFs can also be used to create a synthetic currency loan in a currency that may face liquidity and other issues. For example, a domestic corporation in a country faced with currency market limitations may need to borrow US dollars to pay a supplier, but it has to make repayments in the local currency. Under the terms agreed in the NDF, the borrower receives the

US dollar sum from the lender and repayments are calculated in US dollars, but made in the local currency at an agreed exchange rate. The lender enters into an NDF agreement with another party that matches the cash flow from the original deal based on the foreign currency repayments. The borrower has met their need for a loan in US dollars; the lender has created a synthetic dollar loan; and the counterparty has an NDF contract with the lender.

Tip

These complex deals are usually undertaken for large amounts between governments, large financial institutions, and multinational corporations with global operations and risk exposure.

Swaps

Currency swaps originated in the United Kingdom in the 1970s, when UK companies were forced to pay a premium to borrow US dollars, so they set up back-to-back loans with US companies that needed to borrow British pounds.

Currency swaps are the simultaneous purchase and sale of identical amounts of one currency for another with different value dates. They allow the two parties involved in the swap to exchange aspects of a loan in one currency (the principal and interest payments) for equivalent aspects in another currency.

Swaps can be straightforward currency swaps, where one currency is simply swapped for another currency and then the swap reversed at an agreed future date; they can combine the currency exchange with interest rate and other payments; or they may involve swapping only the interest rate payments on loans of the same size and maturity date. They generally involve a spot transaction combined with a forward outright transaction. Commercial swaps make use of comparative advantage where a domestic borrower may be able to secure a more favourable interest rate than an overseas borrower. The domestic borrower can then swap the principle, or the repayments, or a combination of both, with an offshore party for a similar deal in another currency, offering benefits for both parties.

Tip

Swaps are used by large commercial banks and central banks to fund their foreign exchange balances and to ensure they have access to widely used currencies as and when they need them. Commercial banks use swaps if they need to exchange currencies with other banks or if a client needs a large amount of a currency.

Central banks use swaps to maintain liquidity during times of economic difficulty, such as during the global financial crisis. The aim of these swaps is to maintain liquidity in US dollars in the global banking system. The central banks swap currencies according to their need to make emergency loans using their domestic currency. In this situation they are able to swap their foreign currency reserves of, say, US dollars with the US Federal Reserve Bank's reserves of other currencies.

Large multinational corporations also use swaps to secure cheaper funding or to hedge against exchange rate fluctuations. Cheaper debt funding uses the comparative advantage function described above whereby a local institution borrows funds at the best available rate and then swaps the debt in a back-to-back loan with an offshore company.

A currency hedge can also be put in place to reduce exposure to foreign exchange fluctuations by using a swap in one of two ways. Let's say an Australian-based company needs to borrow euros, and a French company needs to borrow the same amount in Australian dollars. If the two companies have already borrowed the funds in the country where they are required, they could arrange a swap of cash flows so that each company's borrowing cost is now in their domestic currency. Alternatively, they could arrange the loans in their domestic currencies (perhaps with a comparative advantage in regard to interest rates) and then arrange a principal swap into the currency they need.

Tip

Swaps are an over-the-counter product like forwards, so they can be arranged according to the requirements of the parties concerned and are agreed according to these needs. Amounts, repayment dates and all other components of the contract are flexible and can be negotiated between the parties involved.

Currency futures

A futures contract is a legally binding, standardised agreement to buy or sell a standardised commodity or financial instrument of specific quality and quantity on a specified future delivery date at a given location. The only variable is price.

Futures contracts are based on an underlying, tangible commodity, such as wheat or lean hogs, or an index, such as the S&P 500, or, in Australia, the share price index (SPI). Some futures contracts, such as wheat and live cattle, call for physical delivery, while others, such as S&P 500 and SPI contracts, are cash settled. Futures contracts are traded on a regulated exchange. As a derivative product, like all futures contracts, currency futures are traded using leverage, allowing a small amount of capital to control a much larger position.

Similarly, currency futures are futures contracts where the underlying commodity is an exchange rate, such as the

Australian dollar to US dollar exchange rate. A currency futures contract is a contract to exchange one currency for another at a specified future date at an exchange rate that is fixed on the date of the transaction. Currency futures are traded in pairs, with the value of one currency quoted against the value of another. Like all futures contracts, currency futures are standardised contracts, traded on an exchange, and always cash settled, as one currency amount is always exchanged for another.

Tip

Currency futures were introduced by the Chicago Mercantile Exchange (CME) in 1972 following the collapse of the Bretton Woods Accord and the introduction of free-floating currencies, because traders, investors and brokers were frustrated by the lack of access to the inter-bank market for currency trading.

Traders at the CME established the International Money Market (IMM) as an alternative to the inter-bank market and launched trading in seven currency futures, creating a market for standardised futures contracts with a matching and clearing service for the prompt execution of all trades. The IMM operates today as a division of the CME, offering futures contracts in 19 currency pairs, including two e-mini contracts and six e-micro contracts, which are smaller versions of the standard futures contracts. Currency futures are also traded on the New York Stock Exchange (NYSE), the Euronext Exchange in London, the Tokyo Financial Exchange and the Intercontinental Exchange (ICE) based in the US.

Currency futures contract specifications

Like all futures contracts, currency futures have standardised contracts and are traded on a registered exchange. Each contract has detailed specifications, including where and when the contract can be traded, the face value or size of the contract, the smallest incremental price point that can be traded, the date of expiry of the contract, and the margin requirements. Figure 3.1 shows the contract specifications for the New Zealand dollar currency futures contract traded on the CME.

Trading on a registered exchange means that there is no counter party risk for either party involved in a futures transaction. Unlike over-the-counter contracts, such as forwards and swaps, where there is the risk that either party to the deal may default, the risk of default with futures contracts is virtually zero because the buyer and the seller do not deal directly with each other. Instead, the exchange clearing house guarantees both sides of the transaction. The clearing house achieves this by charging traders an initial margin and a maintenance margin on each futures contract. The operation of a centralised exchange is shown in figure 3.2.

Contract prices for futures are determined by the interest rate for the currency pair that constitutes the futures contract, as well as the prevailing spot rate for each currency. This means that any arbitrage differences between the futures market and the spot market are eliminated, as the contract price moves in tandem with fluctuations in the spot rate. The following formula is used to set the price for a contract for a given currency pair:

$$F = S (1 + RQ \times T) \div (1 + RB \times T)$$

Where:

F = the price for the currency futures contract

S = the spot rate for the currency pair

RQ = the interest rate of the quote currency

RB = the interest rate of the base currency

T = the tenor, or time to maturity (in days)

Figure 3.1: contract specifications for New Zealand dollar futures

Contract Size	100,000 New Zealand dollars
Contract Month Listings	Six months in the March quarterly cycle (Mar, Jun, Sep, Dec)
Settlement Procedure	Physical Delivery
Position Accountability	6,000 contracts
Ticker Symbol	CME Globex Electronic Markets: 6N Open Outcry (All-or-None only: NE AON Code: UK View product and vendor codes
Minimum Price Increment	$.0001 per New Zealand dollar increments ($10.00/contract). $.00005 per New Zealand dollar ($5.00/contract) for NZD/USD futures intr-currency spreads executed on the trading floor and electronically, and for AON transactions.

Trading Hours	OPEN OUTCRY (RTH)	7:20 a.m.-2.00 p.m. AON only
	GLOBEX (ETH)	Sundays: 5:00 p.m. – 4:00 p.m. Central Time (CT) next day. Monday – Friday: 5:00 p.m. – 4:00 p.m. CT the next day, except on Friday - closes at 4:00 p.m. and reopens Sunday at 5:00 p.m. CT.
	CME ClearPort	Sunday – Friday 6:00 p.m. – 5:15 p.m. (5:00 p.m. – 4:15 p.m. Chicago Time/CT) with a 45–minute break each day beginning at 5:15 p.m. (4:15 p.m. CT)

Last Trade Date / Time View calendar	9:16 a.m. Central Time (CT) on the second business day immediately preceding the third Wednesday of the contract month (usually Monday).
Exchange Rule	These contracts are listed with, and subject to, the rules and regulations of CME.
Block Trade Eligibility	Yes. View more on Block Trade eligible contracts.
Block Trade Minimum	50 contracts
EFP Eligibility	Yes. View more on EFPs.

Source: CME Group.

Figure 3.2: how a centralised market works

Tip

Price arbitrage can occur when the same currency is listed on more than one exchange at the same time. If the price change on one exchange lags behind the other then an opportunity arises to profit from the difference in price between the two exchanges. If, for example, the value of the Australian dollar rose on the spot market, but this was not reflected in the futures market, then an arbitrage opportunity would exist. If the futures market price were seen to be lagging, then theoretically it would be possible to buy the Australian dollar futures contract in anticipation of it 'catching up' to the price in the spot market.

Currency futures are used by both hedgers and speculators. Importers, exporters and international banks use currency futures to hedge and reduce currency exchange rate exposure. These organisations may have a forward payment due, or be expecting a payment in the future, and they can lock in the exchange rate before the due date through the use of currency futures. Traders seeking to profit from exchange rate movements are also active participants in the currency futures markets. They are attracted to the use of currency futures by the leverage offered, the liquidity available and the ability to trade both long and short in the currency futures market.

The mechanics of trading currency futures will be discussed in detail in chapter 4.

The spot market

The spot foreign exchange market is an inter-bank or inter-dealer electronic, over-the-counter (OTC) network linking currency traders around the globe and around the clock. As an OTC market, transactions do not occur on a central exchange like the CME futures exchange or the Australian Securities

Exchange (ASX), but instead are made electronically between the two parties involved in the transaction. Originally the domain of the large banks and other financial institutions who traded with each other and with other credit-approved institutions, the arrival of the internet and the development of broker and dealer online trading platforms has facilitated the trading of forex by retail clients by computer. Retail traders are now able to trade in the forex inter-bank market through their chosen broker or dealer platform. The operation of the spot market is shown in figure 3.3.

The spot market is also referred to as the foreign exchange market, FX, forex, spot FX, margin FX and retail FX—regardless of the term, the spot market is simply the trading of one currency against the value of another. Currencies are always traded as pairs, with prices based on the spread between these two prices being established by the participants in the market.

Figure 3.3: how the decentralised spot forex market works

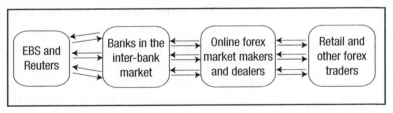

The original purpose of the spot forex market was to support international trade and investment by allowing commercial banks and businesses trading internationally to convert one currency to another. The spot market is now also the largest speculative market in the world, and the world's most liquid and accessible cash market. The spot market is the first step in all international currency flows, as deals can be done within seconds as exchange rates change in line with interest rate and other economic announcements, geo-political events, and a wide variety of other factors. The spot market can be seen as the world's last truly free market.

Tip

A spot foreign exchange transaction involves the purchase of one currency against the sale of another at the current market rate for settlement in two days' time. It is effectively the purchase of one currency by borrowing another.

Currency transactions that require same-day settlement are called cash transactions. The two-day delivery period for spot currency transactions was originally developed long before the information technology systems we now have were available. Two days was seen as a reasonable time for both sides of the transaction to check all the details, rectify any mistakes and then arrange settlement. If a standard spot deal is not settled within two days, interest accrues against the party that has failed to deliver—this is known as rollover or roll. In the retail forex market, open positions (any trades that you have open) are automatically rolled over by your broker to the next settlement day. You may be charged or paid interest depending on your open position. This process forms the basis of the carry trade, which will be discussed in chapter 6.

Tip

The spot forex market originated in 1971, when many of the major world currencies began moving towards free-floating exchange rates. The spot market is therefore considered the oldest foreign exchange market, and it represents the underlying market for all foreign exchange–related derivatives, including currency futures, forwards, swaps and options.

Combined average daily turnover in all OTC forex-related instruments was estimated by the Bank of International Settlements (BIS) Triennial Central Bank Survey in April of 2010 to be US$3.98 trillion. This is a 20 per cent increase over the US$3.32 trillion estimated average daily turnover reported in the same survey in April 2007. This daily turnover is broken down as follows:

⇨ US$1.490 trillion in foreign exchange spot transactions

⇨ US$475 billion in forward contracts

⇨ US$1.765 trillion in forex swap transactions (principal only)

⇨ US$43 billion in currency swaps (interest only)

⇨ US$207 billion in options and other products.

Turnover in the spot market increased by approximately 48 per cent from just over US$1 trillion per day in the April 2007 survey to US$1.49 trillion by April 2010. The spot market now accounts for 37 per cent of OTC daily foreign exchange turnover, just behind the swaps market, which accounts for 45 per cent of the average daily OTC foreign exchange turnover. The average daily turnover in the OTC swaps market increased by just under 4 per cent over the same three-year period. These figures highlight the enormous growth that has occurred in the spot forex market.

The growth in the global foreign exchange market and, in particular, the spot market since 1998 is shown in table 3.1 (overleaf). Also of interest is the growth in the average daily turnover of exchange-traded derivatives (currency futures) over this period. From a relatively small US$11 billion per day in 1998, turnover has grown to US$166 billion per day in 2010. In the three-year period from 2007 to 2010, average daily turnover in currency futures increased by over 107 per cent.

Table 3.1: average daily global foreign exchange market turnover in April, 1998 to 2010, in billions of US dollars

Instrument	1998	2001	2004	2007	2010
Spot transactions	568	386	631	1005	1490
Forward outrights	128	130	209	362	475
Forex swaps (principal only)	734	656	954	1714	1765
Currency swaps	10	7	21	31	43
Options and other	87	60	119	212	207
Total of OTC forex instruments	1527	1239	1934	3324	3981
Exchange traded products	11	12	26	80	166

Source: Bank of International Settlements Triennial Central Bank Survey, April 2010.

The geographical spread of traders participating in the spot market has led to the emergence of major trading centres covering the major world time zones, even though foreign exchange can be traded 24 hours a day for five and a half days per week, starting in New Zealand on Monday morning (Sydney time) and finishing with the close of the New York market early Saturday morning Sydney time. According to the BIS Triennial Study in 2010, banks located in the UK accounted for almost 37 per cent of average daily turnover. This was followed by the US with 18 per cent; Japan, 6 per cent; Singapore, Switzerland and Hong Kong, 5 per cent each; and Australia, 4 per cent. Since London is the major foreign exchange market, most online trading platforms tend to use the buy and sell prices being quoted in London.

Chapter summary

⇨ As well as the central banks, which have a role in and influence on the global foreign exchange market, many other participants are involved in trading foreign exchange.

⇨ Major international banks deal either directly with each other or through two main electronic platforms, EBS and Reuters, which offer trading in the major currency pairs.

⇨ The inter-bank market is a wholesale market that is unregulated and decentralised, and it operates around the world and around the clock.

⇨ Much of the activity of large multinational companies in the foreign exchange market involves hedging against adverse currency movements to protect their overseas and import and export operations, or locking in favourable exchange rates, though many also speculate in the currency markets.

⇨ Hedge funds are becoming increasingly involved in the foreign exchange market, attracted by the leverage it offers to increase returns on their funds under management.

⇨ The development of the internet and the advent of online trading platforms have revolutionised trading for retail and private traders in investors across all markets.

⇨ Retail and small traders provide liquidity and price discovery to the market, making it easier for hedgers and arbitrageurs to offset their risk. Retail and small traders are the largest section by number within the overall foreign exchange market.

⇨ Forwards are a non-standardised contract between two parties to buy or sell a specified amount of a currency at an agreed exchange rate (called the delivery price) at an agreed future date.

⇨ A non-deliverable forward (NDF) is similar to a forward outright, except that no physical delivery of the principal or notional amount takes place. Only the difference between the two prices is exchanged in cash.

⇨ Currency swaps are the simultaneous purchase and sale of identical amounts of one currency for another with different value dates.

⇨ Currency futures are futures contracts where the underlying commodity is an exchange rate, such as the Australian dollar to US dollar exchange rate.

⇨ The spot market is also referred to as the foreign exchange market, FX, forex, spot FX, margin FX and retail FX. Regardless of the term, the spot market is simply the trading of one currency against the value of another.

⇨ The original purpose of the spot forex market was to encourage international trade and investment by allowing commercial banks and businesses trading internationally to convert one currency to another. Spot forex is now also the largest speculative market in the world, and the world's most liquid and accessible cash market.

chapter 4

Retail forex dealers and market makers

The spot forex market has opened up to retail traders like us since the inception of the internet and the development of online broker trading platforms. These provide access to the currencies and prices traded on the inter-bank market through a network of dealers and market makers. Before we rip into the actual how-to-do-it part of forex trading, it is important to understand how the market works, how prices are quoted and orders placed, and how the foreign exchange platform providers make their money.

Forex market structure

Before the development of the internet, the forex market was the domain of the large commercial banks, large financial institutions, hedge funds and large multinational corporations. It was essentially a relatively small group of large players interacting with each other in a closed shop that was based upon credit agreements among the participants. The market was not regulated and while the seemingly ad-hoc approach of those days may seem bizarre to those who are more familiar with trading on a regulated exchange, such as the ASX, CME or NYSE, it actually functioned very efficiently.

Tip

Because the major participants in the forex market compete and cooperate with each other, this self-regulation tends to ensure that no-one acts to the disadvantage of any other player.

The first significant change to this cosy model occurred in 1992 with the introduction of electronic dealing platforms. These allowed inter-bank traders to interact electronically rather than dealing with each other over the phone or by cable, which increased the speed with which orders could be executed and allowed a wider and deeper trading environment. The ability to trade online by means of a trading platform also meant that forex could now be made available to a much wider trading base. Enter some progressive and forward-thinking market makers and dealers, and the retail forex trading revolution was born.

It is best to imagine the spot forex market as having a two-tiered structure. Tier one, or the top level, consists of the large banks and other financial institutions that are constantly dealing with each other on behalf of themselves or their clients in the inter-bank market. At this level, quantities traded are large, often in the millions and even billions of dollars, and the price spread between the buy and the sell price is extremely tight. Prices quoted in this inter-bank market are known only to the participants and are not available elsewhere. The inter-bank market still functions as a credit-approved system in which the banks trade based on the credit relationships they have in place with each other. The bigger banks will have more and larger credit relationships, and access to better pricing and tighter bid/ask spreads. The large commercial banks operating in this tier are the primary market makers for the foreign exchange market.

Tip

A market maker is an organisation that continuously quotes buy and sell prices in the market and is always willing and able to deal at these quoted prices.

This market-making role ensures there is always a price to trade at, and it provides continuous liquidity for the market. The fact that a number of banks are prepared to assume the role of market maker creates an efficient market, because large price discrepancies do not occur. Market making also effectively creates the market, as the inter-bank dealers buy and sell among themselves in order to profit from these slight variations in price. These variations in price arise because each bank will have a different view on the direction they think a foreign exchange rate will move. Banks will also be holding varying amounts, or inventory positions, of different currencies depending on their own needs and the requirements of their clients. The bank dealers may, for example, believe that the Canadian dollar is about to rise in value against the US dollar because of events in the oil and energy markets. The dealers may be willing to offer a higher bid or buy price for Canadian dollars to encourage someone else to sell to them, as they believe that they can hold these Canadian dollars for a while and then sell them out again at a higher price. On the flip side, if their analysis suggests to them that the Canadian dollar is about to fall they will lower their bid price as they don't really want to buy and have to sell out of the position later at a lower price. This ability to vary both buy and sell prices, and therefore the spread, or difference between the buy and sell price, is unique to market makers and is possible because they are continuously quoting both bid (or buy) and offer (or sell) prices in the market.

The second tier, or level, of forex is the retail forex market. At this level, retail traders gain access to the market through dealer-based electronic trading platforms. Retail forex dealers can get access to the market on behalf of their clients according to their size and the credit relationships they have with the major banks in the inter-bank market. Working in a similar way to the inter-bank market, at this level the larger the retail forex dealer is in terms of capital available and creditworthiness, the more favourable the pricing and bid/ask spreads it will receive from the inter-bank market. A small retail forex dealer with fewer credit relationships will be restricted to dealing with a limited number of the larger banks and will get less favourable prices and spreads than a larger operator.

Tip

The quotes and spreads offered at the retail level are not the same as those within the inter-bank market, but will very closely resemble them.

The banks providing quotes to the retail forex dealers may widen the spreads or add a margin to the buy/sell quotes to assist in their risk management and also to make a profit.

Retail forex dealers

If you already trade shares or futures you no doubt have a broker who acts as an agent for you in your trading transactions. The broker accepts your order, either by phone or over an electronic online platform, and then sends the order to the exchange, where the order is executed according to your instructions. In return for this service, the broker charges you a commission. The broker's only role is to accept your order, place it in the market, and charge you for doing so.

The forex market works differently. Unlike the traditional exchange-based markets on which shares and futures are traded, the forex market, as we have discussed, is essentially a principals-only market. To gain access to the market, participants must have suitable amounts of capital available and have credit relationships in place to get access to the inter-bank market. Participants then trade as the principal in each deal. For example, let's assume that a large bank client needs to buy US$20 million of euro currency. The bank would buy the euros in the inter-bank market on their own account, acting as principal for the trade, and then provide the euro currency to their client.

At the retail level a similar process occurs, with the firm where your account is held acting as the principal for your trade within the inter-bank market as either a market maker or dealer. Your order is not sent into the inter-bank market as an order to buy, say, 20 000 worth of euro currency for Mr Fred Jones; it is seen in the market as just another order for a firm acting as the principal. It is then allocated to your account by the firm where your account is held. All this takes place within a few seconds through the electronic platforms, dealing desks and computer-operated matching systems that constitute the foreign exchange market.

Tip

The firm where your retail forex account is held will operate in the market as either a market maker or dealer. It is important to understand the differences between each and how the different operations affect your trading and your bottom line.

Market makers or dealing desks

Retail forex market makers have a slightly different role than that played by the banks as market makers in the inter-bank market, where market makers function to provide continuing buy and sell prices, and provide liquidity for the market. Retail forex market-maker firms will maintain bid/ask prices and will be willing and able to deal with clients at these publicly quoted prices. These prices are *not* the prices operating in the inter-bank market and may not match them at all, as they are derived from the underlying instrument. The market maker may add several price points to the buy and sell prices, and may also widen the spread between the two prices, sometimes significantly, and that is how they make their money.

When an order is received from a client the market maker may, however, take a number of different actions:

⇨ *Take the other side of the order.* When an order is received from a client, the client is actually buying from or selling to the market maker. If the client buys, the market maker sells from their inventory; if the client sells, the market maker buys by effectively lending the client inventory until the position is closed. When the client loses on a trade, the market maker profits, and vice versa. The market maker may or may not lay-off the risk, by placing the trade in the actual market, depending on their view of market direction and their knowledge of the client's trading history. If it is a client with a history of losing trades, the market maker will more often than not bet against the client and not hedge the position. If it is a larger, more successful client, they may well hedge the position in the market and take the risk out of the trade.

⇨ *Delay matching orders.* Once the client order is placed and filled, the market maker may wait anywhere from a few seconds to minutes before they then trade at a better price. When the client closes the order, the market maker may again wait and close the order out at a better price. This strategy works for the market maker most of the time because of the high losing trade rate among retail forex traders and the high percentage of retail trades and order flows that are placed in a counter-trend fashion.

⇨ *Consolidate smaller orders.* The market maker may wait until a number of smaller client orders are placed before laying-off the position in the market. The small lot sizes will be traded on the market maker's platform prices, which may be different from those trading on the actual market, allowing the market maker to profit from the price difference.

⇨ *Match buyers and sellers internally.* The market maker may simply match a buy order for a currency from one client with a sell order for the same currency from another client. This can happen on a continuing basis throughout the day as buy and sell orders are received as clients trade in and out of positions. The market maker may be left with some small positions at the end of each day, which they then offset in the market by buying or selling currency to ensure they have no open positions to nullify any exposure or risk.

Tip

Typically, market makers do not charge commissions or add an advertised mark-up to the prices quoted on their platforms because they are profiting from their client's activities in other ways, as discussed above.

While commission-free trading may seem appealing it must be remembered that there is no such thing as a free lunch in this world—particularly in trading. You *will* pay a fee to trade, but how you pay it will vary. The market maker widening the spread between the bid and ask prices is one way they can make a profit, and your profitability can be reduced. If the market maker widens a spread from three points to say five, the cost to you has increased by two points, or 66 per cent. By way of example, let's assume you are trading at $5 per pip. (The way forex trading works is explained in detail in chapter 5, providing you with a full understanding of pips, spreads and all the other information you need to trade forex. This example is included here to highlight the fact that trading is rarely 'free' and that the trader will incur costs somehow.) With the increase in the spread, it will now effectively cost you $25 to enter a trade (5 pips at $5 per pip = $25), and it will also cost you $25 to exit the trade (if the 5 pip spread remains the same) because you have to cross the spread in order for your trade to be executed. A total cost of $50 — that's hardly a free trade. Spreads for cross rates and exotic currency pair combinations may be much higher.

Market makers will generally manage the risk of a pool of many traders rather than the profit and loss of every individual account by managing the net position of all long (buy) positions and all short (sell) positions in each currency pair. A team of internal traders and dealers will manage the net position as if it were one large trading account. Market makers may still, however, offset individual trades in the inter-bank market, depending on the profitability of the individual trader. Consistently profitable traders can be placed on a separate trade server that provides automatic execution and allows their trades to be offset in the inter-bank market, thus de-risking each trade for the market maker, while they still make money on the spread.

A pool of consistently unprofitable traders who are losing money can be managed internally by the market maker's dealers and traders without offsetting each trade in the inter-bank market. As the market maker is the counterparty to the client's trades, a loss for the trader represents profit for the market maker. If a client opens a $10 000 trading account and loses the lot through poor risk management, then the market maker has made $10 000 profit. If this occurs to 50 traders in a 12-month period, then the market maker has the potential to earn $500 000, just by taking the other side of the positions of these losing traders.

Tip

While market makers don't want to see their clients lose money, it's obvious that losing traders enhance the market maker's bottom line. It is this conflict of interest that contributes to some bad press and negative sentiment for the market-maker model.

Retail forex dealers or non-dealing desks

Retail forex dealers operate in a similar way to brokers in other markets, except that they are dealing as the principal. Their role is to serve as an agent of the client in the broader forex market by seeking the best price in the market for the client's order and then dealing on behalf of the client. Unlike market makers, retail dealers charge a commission or mark-up on the market price. They are known as non-dealing desk (NDD) firms or direct market access (DMA) firms. These firms access the forex market through an electronic communication network (ECN) that matches orders from retail traders with prices supplied by the inter-bank market makers or banks. The infrastructure for these firms consists of a computer-based trading screen, or front end, and an application programming interface (API) that distributes the prices and available quantities from contributing banks.

Tip

An API is a software program interface that allows interaction between different software programs. Its use means that the software program the retail forex firm provides and the client users on their laptop or home computer can interact with the various software programs the inter-bank market makers use to provide prices to the retail forex firm.

The retail forex firm receives price quotes and quantities that the quote is good, or available, from the bank market makers in the forex market. These prices also have a duration, or length of time for which they are good, or available. A sort engine then sorts out the best bids and offers, and quotes these on the retail client's software program. This process is happening continually whenever the forex market is open.

It is here that the size and creditworthiness of the retail forex firm becomes important for its clients. The larger the capitalisation of the firm and the better its credit rating, the more banks it will have access to. This means it will have access to a wider range of prices and price spreads in the market and will be better able to serve the needs of its clients. As the banks are competing for your business, the greater the number of banks, the greater the competition among them to offer better prices and tighter bid/ask spreads. It also means trades can be executed more quickly, as there are more price quotes being offered by the different banks from which to choose the best bid or offer at any one time. The retail firm FXCM, for example, has access to prices provided by 11 top tier banks.

Once the retail forex firm receives the price quotes, and while they are being sorted according to the best available price, a mark-up, or margin, is added to the price by the dealer *before* the price is quoted to the retail client on their trading platform. When we, as retail clients, see a price on our trading platforms, we see the price from the bank that currently has the best bid or offer, *plus* the mark-up charged by the dealer.

Tip

The mark-up is the commission charged by the non-dealing desk (NDD) or direct market access (DMA) firm, and it's how they make their money.

Other features of trading with a DMA or NDD retail forex firm include:

⇨ *anonymity.* Because the DMA or NDD firm is acting as principal for all the retail traders that are its clients, orders appear in the bank market as coming from the retail forex firm, and not from individual clients' accounts. Client orders to buy or sell remain on the retail forex firm's server and are sent into the market electronically as market orders once the price has been reached. The banks can't see where the orders are sitting. The downside is that in a fast-moving market the retail client will experience slippage (see tip overleaf).

⇨ *no maximum trade size.* While the retail forex market makers may impose trade size limitations because of the risks for them in taking the opposing side of large positions, DMA or NDD forex dealers will, as a general rule, accept large order sizes, up to US$50 million per trade, through their electronic trading platforms. This limitation will not adversely affect the majority of online retail forex traders. Multiple parcels of orders of this size, or large single orders, can be placed by telephoning these orders through to the dealing desk.

⇨ *variable price spreads.* As they are providing price quotes direct from a number of providers that are constantly ebbing and flowing and being 'sorted' for the best available deal, it is natural that the price spreads will vary in line with supply and demand and other economic and news events that continually cause changes in price.

⇨ *no price requotes.* A price requote is said to occur when an order is not filled at the requested price and the trader is offered another, different price. A requote may be the result of a slow transfer of data and price information, or a liquidity-related issue where the amount requested is unavailable at the requested price, or the result of trading in a fast-moving market where the dealing firm may be exposed to a larger risk than normal by their holding a price for too long. DMA or NDD dealers will fill orders at the next available price, rather than offer requotes.

Tip

Slippage occurs when a resting stop or limit order is filled several pips above or below the required price. Once a stop or limit order price is triggered, it then becomes an at market or at best order, and it will be filled at the next available price. In a fast-moving, volatile market, or in cases where liquidity is temporarily reduced, this may result in the position being filled at a significantly different rate than the one requested. Slippage can occur in all markets, not just the forex market.

Choosing a retail forex dealer that suits you

When assessing the forex dealer you will trade with, it is important to choose a reputable dealing firm that is well capitalised, has strong relationships with the banks and can deliver the liquidity you need to trade effectively. You also need to know and understand the impact on your trading of all fees, charges, commissions and costs.

Tip

In choosing your dealer you also need to consider the ramifications of both types of service provider—market maker or non-dealing desk—as discussed above. When dealing with a market maker, no commission is payable, but you may not be getting the best price available, and the service provider, by taking the opposite side of your trade, has a conflict of interest in your success as a trader. The direct market access (DMA) dealer charges commission or mark-up on each trade, so the more you trade and the more profitable you become, the more commission they can earn.

Having identified and chosen the type of service provider you want to trade with—market maker or DMA, and the cost structure, fees and commissions they charge—following are six important points to consider when selecting the retail forex firm with which you chose to trade.

Are they regulated? If so, in which country?

While the spot forex operates as an over-the-counter market that is mostly self-regulated and subject to little government or exchange regulation, it is important for a retail trader to choose a foreign exchange dealer firm that is based in a country where their overall activities and licensing arrangements are subject to regulations and monitored by a regulatory agency.

Tip

A dealer located in a country without strict regulatory guidelines will not be subject to the same trade and credit control rules as one that is.

The major forex trading countries that have regulatory bodies, and the bodies that regulate them, include:

⇨ Australia — Australian Securities & Investments Commission (ASIC)

⇨ United States — Commodities and Futures Trading Commission (CFTC); Securities and Exchanges Commission (SEC); National Futures Association (NFA)

⇨ United Kingdom — Financial Services Authority

⇨ Eurozone — Markets in Financial Instruments Directive (MiFID)

⇨ Canada — Investment Industry Regulatory Organization of Canada (IIROC)

⇨ Japan — Financial Services Agency (FSA); Financial Futures Association of Japan (FFAJ); Japan Security Dealers Association (JSDA)

⇨ Switzerland — Swiss Financial Market Supervisory Authority (FINMA).

Regulatory authorities are located in many other countries, and traders need to be aware of their dealer's regulatory status.

What is their capitalisation?

The better capitalised retail forex dealer firms are (in other words the more they are worth and the more money they have as working capital), the more credit relationships they are able to establish with the banks and other liquidity providers, and the more competitive pricing and spreads they are able to achieve for their clients. This also means that, under volatile market conditions, they will be able to offer continuous pricing without the need to requote.

The OTC nature of the spot forex market requires the retail forex firms to deposit an amount of money (referred to as margin) with the banks that provide prices and spreads to them. Obviously, the more capital the retail firm has, the more banks they can deposit margin with in order to secure credit and trading relationships.

Tip

A retail forex firm that is not well capitalised would find it difficult to remain competitive in the market.

In the US, dealers are required to be members of regulatory associations. As a member of a regulatory body, a dealer must comply with minimum capitalisation levels. As at June 2010, this figure was set at US$20 million. If a dealer does not make information about the regulatory requirement of capitalisation available to clients and doesn't meet the requirements, that may indicate a lack of solvency.

How user-friendly and reliable is their trading platform?

The online trading platform supplied by your chosen broker is your interface with the forex market, so it needs to be both simple and easy to use, yet still offer all the necessary features and tools you need, and be easy to navigate around to access these features. Features may include the provision of news and other information, real-time or live price charts and charting tools, economic data and access to prices on important commodities, such as gold and oil.

Tip

The ability to open and close trades quickly is a major consideration in choosing your broker. The steps needed to place buy and sell orders, as well as any stop and limit entry and exit orders, should also be a simple process. In a fast-moving, volatile market you need to be able to place orders with as few mouse clicks as possible. Slow trade entry and order execution may result in lost opportunities.

The platform also needs to be very stable, and not crash or freeze up. This is particularly important during times of increased activity around major news events and announce-ments, when trading activity may spike suddenly. The reliability of the platform to hold up under pressure and not lock up is perhaps even more important than the look and feel of the platform.

While these features are important to all traders, they are essential for short-term or aggressive traders who make frequent trades and need to enter and exit trades quickly and efficiently. Seconds lost navigating around a clunky platform can prove costly, and so can platform crashes or freezes. These issues are less important, though still relevant, to a more conservative, medium-term trader who may buy and sell on stop and limit orders, rather than market orders. The various order types used are discussed in chapter 6.

We will also take a more detailed look at trading platforms and how to use them in chapter 5.

What customer support do they provide?

The 24-hour nature of the forex market and the fact that no matter what your time zone you can choose to trade whenever it suits you, should also mean that your provider has a 24-hour support desk. Just because it is the middle of the day in Sydney and night-time in the northern hemisphere doesn't mean you should not have access to customer support for your technical and account-related questions. You need prompt answers to any issues that arise. You should not have to wait hours until the support desk on the other side of the world opens at 9.00 am New York time, or the accounts department in the Singapore office turn up for work. Nor should you have access to customer support only during the daylight hours of the city of the company's head office. The forex market runs 24 hours a day, so customer support needs to be the same. The retail forex dealer firms that are serious about their client relationships make 24-hour support available.

You also need to know how you can contact the support desk and what means of communication are available. This should include email and live chat, as well as being able to speak on the telephone. Support must be available in your language so that problems and issues are clearly understood and then rectified.

What types of accounts do they offer?

As well as standard accounts, many retail forex firms also offer small mini accounts and smaller micro accounts. A standard account trades standard lots of $100 000 face-value positions, and multiples of $100 000; a mini account trades mini lots of $10 000 face-value positions and multiples of $10 000; and a micro account trades micro lots of $1000 face-value and multiples of $1000. Mini and micro accounts allow traders with small amounts of capital to participate in the forex market by reducing their risk and exposure through smaller position sizes and trade values. You will need to check that your chosen provider offers the type of account that is the best fit for the amount of capital you have available.

What leverage is offered and what is their margin call policy?

A detailed discussion of leverage and margin follows in chapter 5. The important things to consider when selecting your forex dealer are the leverage levels they offer and whether these levels are fixed or variable, depending on the currency being traded. Some traders may choose their dealer based on the high leverage levels offered without understanding the implications of incorrectly using leverage. While high leverage can lead to higher profits and greater percentage returns on available capital, it also increases the level of risk. The misuse of high levels of leverage is one of the main reasons new traders fail in their attempts to trade forex.

It is also important to understand the margin call policy of your retail forex firm. If you do get a margin call through over-exposure and poor money management, you need to know how the dealer will handle your account. Some firms use the first-in-first-out (FIFO) method to close trades when margin requirements fall short of current available equity — that means they will close out older positions first in order to reinstate margin requirement levels. Other firms use the last-in-first-out (LIFO) method, meaning they will close the most recent trades first. Other firms will simply close all trades. This is another area that you need to identify and clarify before you start trading.

The structure of the spot forex market, and the main differences between dealers and how they make their money, have now been outlined. In the next chapter we will examine all the other information you need to know about the spot forex market.

Chapter summary

⇨ Before the development of the internet, the forex market was the domain of the large commercial banks, large financial institutions, hedge funds and large multinational corporations.

⇨ It is best to think of the spot forex market as having a two-tier structure. Tier one, or the top level, is made up of the large banks and other financial institutions constantly dealing between each other, on their own behalf or on behalf of their clients in the inter-bank market. The second tier, or lower level, is the retail forex market. At this level, retail traders gain access to the forex market through dealer-based electronic trading platforms.

⇨ Unlike the traditional exchange-based markets on which shares and futures are traded, the forex market is essentially a principals only market. To gain access to the market, participants must have suitable amounts of capital available and have credit relationships in place in order to be able to gain access to the inter-bank market.

⇨ Retail forex brokers are either market makers or non-dealing desk firms.

⇨ Market makers generally act as the counterparty to their clients' trades by taking the opposite side of the trade.

⇨ Non-dealing desk firms act as an agent for the client, transacting in the inter-bank market on behalf of the client.

⇨ Retail traders need to carefully choose a reputable dealing firm that is well capitalised, has strong relationships with the banks, and can deliver the liquidity they need to trade effectively. Retail traders also need to know and understand the impact of all fees, charges, commissions and costs on their trading.

⇨ It is important for retail traders to spend time researching the different retail forex dealers and seeking out the information they need to make an informed decision on which firm they will choose to trade with.

chapter 5

The mechanics of trading forex

Let's now take a detailed look at the specific information you need to know to trade the spot forex market with confidence, to fully understand what the market is, how to trade, and the unique aspects of the forex market.

Trading forex is trading money

Forex trading is the simultaneous buying of one currency and the selling of another. Currencies are traded through a retail forex dealer, and are traded in pairs: for example, the Australian dollar and the US dollar (AUD/USD) or the euro and the Japanese yen (EUR/JPY). Buying a currency is like buying a share in a particular country. When you buy Australian dollars, for example, you are in effect buying a share in the Australian economy.

The forex spot market does not have a physical location or central exchange where buying and selling takes place, or through which all trades are executed. It is an off-exchange or over-the-counter (OTC) market place where buyers and sellers interact with each other electronically through a network of banks, financial institutions, dealers and other market participants.

Until the late 1990s, only the big guys could participate in forex trading. The initial requirement for trading in forex was a trading account of more than US$10 million. That meant the forex market was used only by banks, governments and other large financial institutions, and not by smaller retail traders and speculators. The development of the internet, the free floating of currencies and developments in technology have allowed forex trading firms and brokers to offer trading accounts to retail traders like you and me.

Tip

All the major currencies are assigned a three-letter abbreviation expressed using International Organization for Standardization (ISO) codes for each currency.

The ISO codes for many of the major world currencies are listed in table 5.1.

Table 5.1: ISO currency codes for major trading currencies

Currency name	ISO code
Australian dollar	AUD
British pound	GBP
Canadian dollar	CAD
Chinese yuan	CNY
European Union euro	EUR
Japanese yen	JPY
New Zealand dollar	NZD
Singapore dollar	SGD
Swedish krona	SEK
Swiss franc	CHF
US dollar	USD

The mechanics of forex trading

An exchange rate is simply the ratio of one currency against the value of another. The NZD/USD exchange rate, for example, indicates what the New Zealand dollar is worth when compared to the US dollar. Currencies are always quoted in pairs because in every foreign exchange transaction you are simultaneously buying one currency and selling another, or exchanging the value of one currency for that of another. This exchange of values is unique to the forex market and can be a little daunting to get your head around initially.

In the sharemarket or futures market when you buy a share or a commodity, your expectation is for the value to increase, allowing you to sell for a profit. If you buy 1000 shares in a company at $5.00 per share and the price increases to $5.50 per share you have made a profit of 50 cents per share, or $500.00 (1000 shares × 50 cents per share). To bank the profit, you simply sell the shares to whoever is willing to pay $5.50 per share.

In the forex market if you anticipate the value of the Australian dollar will rise, what is it going to rise in value against? As it cannot simply rise in value against itself; it has to increase in value relative to the value of another currency, such as the US dollar. If the value of the Australian dollar has risen against the US dollar, then it follows that the value of the US dollar has declined relative to the Australian dollar. If we think of it in terms of the share market, when we buy shares we are selling our cash, and when we sell shares we are buying cash.

Base and quote (or counter) currencies

Currencies are always quoted in pairs. The first currency in the pair is known as the base currency. It is the currency you are buying or selling and is the basis for the transaction. It also represents the face value, or notional, amount of the transaction. If you buy 100 000 NZD/USD, for example, you have just bought 100 000 New Zealand dollars and sold the equivalent amount of US dollars.

The second currency in the pair is called the quote currency or sometimes the counter currency. The quote currency represents the denomination of the price fluctuations and your profit and losses on the trade. So, as with our New Zealand dollar example above, you would actually be buying NZD100 000 worth of New Zealand dollars and selling the equivalent amount of US dollars, and your profit or loss on the trade would be recorded in US dollars.

Tip

Currencies are always traded in pairs.

As an example, if the NZD/USD exchange rate is 0.7500, you would be buying NZD100 000 worth of New Zealand dollars at a rate of 0.7500, and at the same time selling USD133 333 (NZD100 000 divided by 0.7500). In other words, we have to pay 0.7500 US dollars to buy 1 New Zealand dollar. In order for us to make a profit, the value of the New Zealand dollar must rise in value relative to the US dollar.

Tip

The currency listed on the left of the slash (/) is the base currency, and the currency on the right is the quote currency.

Currency pairs

The most actively traded currency pairs are referred to as the majors and generally involve the US dollar on one side of the deal. The major US dollar currency pairs are listed in table 5.2. These are the seven most actively traded currency pairs.

Table 5.2: major US dollar currency pairs

Currency pair	Countries	Name	Nickname
EUR/USD	Eurozone/US	Euro–dollar	Fibre
USD/JPY	US/Japan	Dollar–yen	Yen
USD/CAD	US/Canada	Dollar–Cad	Loonie
AUD/USD	Australia/US	Aussie–dollar	Aussie
GBP/USD	UK/US	Pound–dollar	Cable
USD/CHF	US/Switzerland	Dollar–Swiss	Swissy
NZD/USD	NZ/US	New Zealand–dollar	Kiwi

Tip

Any currency pair that does not involve the US dollar is referred to as a cross currency pair, cross rate or cross.

Cross rates are derived from the respective US dollar–related pairs but are quoted independently. The EUR/JPY cross rate, for example, is derived from the EUR/USD exchange rate and the USD/JPY exchange rate. Cross rates enable trading of currency pairs that may have a unique relationship between countries, such as the AUD/JPY where imports and exports between the two countries don't need to include the US dollar. Cross rates also allow us to target trading opportunities that may exist in specific currency pairs and to take advantage of price patterns, economic data or news events that impact specifically on these cross currency pairs. Some of the most actively traded currency crosses are shown in table 5.3 (overleaf).

The seven major currency pairs listed in table 5.2 and the nine cross currency pairs listed in table 5.3 account for more than 90 per cent of all currency trading activity across all currency trading markets and instruments.

Table 5.3: actively traded currency crosses

Currency pair	Countries	Name
EUR/GBP	Eurozone/UK	Euro–pound
EUR/JPY	Eurozone/Japan	Euro–yen
EUR/CHF	Eurozone/Switzerland	Euro–swissy
GBP/JPY	UK/Japan	Pound–yen
AUD/JPY	Australia/Japan	Aussie–yen
NZD/JPY	New Zealand/Japan	Kiwi–yen
AUD/NZD	Australia/NZ	Aussie–kiwi
AUD/EUR	Australia/Eurozone	Aussie–euro
GBP/AUD	UK/Australia	Pound–aussie

Long or short?

As in any trading, when you are buying to open a trade you are going long and when you are selling to open a trade you are going short.

If you buy the currency pair—that is, buy the base currency and sell the quote currency—you want the base currency to rise in value so you can then sell it at a higher price and make a profit.

If you short sell the currency pair—that is, sell the base currency and buy the quote currency—you want the base currency to fall in value so you can then buy it back at a lower price and make a profit.

Tip

Buying to open is called going long or taking a long position. Selling to open is called going short, shorting or taking a short position.

Understanding pips

A pip is the smallest incremental price move of a currency pair. PIP stands for percentage in point or price interest point. In forex, prices are quoted to four decimal points so the change in the fourth decimal point is equal to one-thousandth of the rate or 0.0001 or 0.01 per cent, hence the term percentage in point. If, for example, the GBP/USD is quoted at 1.5715, then the smallest move it can make to the upside is 1.5716 (1.5715 + 0.0001) and the smallest move it can make to the downside is 1.5714 (1.5717 − 0.0001)—that is, a 1 pip move in either direction.

The exception to this rule is any currency pair involving the Japanese yen where the price quotes are taken to only two decimal places, or one-hundredth of the rate, as the yen has a lower unit value than the other major currencies. If, for example, the USD/JPY is quoted at 83.45, then the smallest move it can make to the upside is 83.46 (83.34 + 0.01) and the smallest move it can make to the downside is 83.44 (83.45 − 0.01)—that is, a 1 pip move in either direction.

Here are listed some currency pair values with the pip show in bold:

AUD/USD: 0.981**8**

EUR/USD: 1.330**4**

USD/JPY: 83.3**7**

USD/CAD: 1.028**6**

Tip

The pip is the last whole number in the quoted price.

In forex, trading profits and losses are measured in pips, so it is important to understand what a pip is.

Pips are used in forex trading because there is no one currency in which values can be indicated and because we are measuring the value of one currency relative to the value of another. Although the US dollar is the most widely traded currency and is traded against most other currencies, it is not involved in all trades. Pip values can be calculated for any currency pair in values that are relevant to each particular pair and are calculated in units of the quote currency, rather than in US dollars. Some examples include euro/Japanese yen (EUR/JPY)—pip values calculated in yen; euro/British pound (EUR/GBP)—pip values calculated in British pounds; and Australian dollar/New Zealand dollar (AUD/NZD)—pip values calculated in NZ dollars.

Tip

The monetary value of a pip changes according to the currencies involved in a trade.

Lot sizes

Spot forex is traded in lots. In order to profit from the tiny pip increments described above, you need to be able to trade large amounts of a currency pair in order to see any substantial profit or loss. If you just went long 1 Aussie dollar (buying AUD/USD) at 0.9885, for example, and the price went up to 0.9890, an increase of 5 pips, you have made 0.0005 cents on the trade—not worth the effort. But because the forex market trades in lots, you are able to significantly magnify this result. Let's take a look at what happens when you buy or sell lots of varying sizes.

The lot size you are able to trade will depend on the amount of capital you have available in your trading account, your risk profile, and the amount of leverage you are able to apply to your account. Leverage will be discussed in more detail later in this chapter.

Tip

A standard lot is 100 000 units of the base currency.

A mini lot is 10 000 units of the base currency.

A micro lot is 1000 units of the base currency.

We now need to combine our knowledge of pips and pip values with the lot size we are trading to determine the dollar value of each pip and to allow us to calculate profit and loss.

Example 1

Let's continue with the Aussie dollar example, going long at 0.9885 in anticipation of a rise in the value of the Aussie dollar relative to the US dollar.

Using a standard lot: you buy 100 000 Aussie dollars and sell 101 163 US dollars.

Using a mini lot: you buy 10 000 Aussie dollars and sell 10 116 US dollars.

Using a micro lot: you buy 1000 Aussie dollars and sell 1012 US dollars.

Solution

To determine the dollar value of each pip, divide the minimum pip move by the exchange rate.

You have bought AUD/USD at 0.9885.

0.0001/0.9885 = AUD 0.000101.

Now multiply this result by the lot size to determine the dollar value of each pip.

For a standard lot, AUD0.000101 × 100 000 = AUD10.10.

As the Aussie dollar is the base currency, we can convert the pip value into US dollars by multiplying the Aussie dollar pip value by the exchange rate.

AUD10.10 × 0.9885 = USD9.98, rounded up = USD10.00 per pip.

The same process can be followed to determine the pip values for mini and micro lots, arriving at USD1.00 for mini lots of 10 000 and USD0.099 (10 cents) for micro lots.

An increase in the price of the AUD/USD pair from 0.9885 to 0.9890, or 5 pips, would increase our return from a measly 0.0005 cents to:

USD50.00 for a standard lot (5 pips × USD10.00 per pip)
USD5.00 for a mini lot (5 pips × USD1.00 per pip)
USD0.50 for a micro lot (5 pips × USD0.10 per pip)

The actions involved in this trade are shown in table 5.4.

Table 5.4: profit calculation using a standard lot

Action	Aussie dollar	US dollar
Buy 100 000 AUD at AUD/USD 0.9885	100 000.00	−101 163.00
Sell 100 000 AUD at AUD/USD 0.9890	−100 000.00	101 113.00
Profit		50.00

Example 2

Any currency pair that has the US dollar as the base currency does not require the step to convert back to US dollars because the initial calculation is in US dollars. Let's work through an example of buying USD/CAD at 1.0285, where the US dollar is the base currency.

Solution

0.0001/1.0285 = 0.0000972.

Multiply by the lot size to determine pip value in dollars.
For a standard lot US$0.0000972 × 100 000 = US$9.72.
For a mini lot US$0.0000972 × 10 000 = US$0.972.
For a micro lot US$0.0000972 × 1000 = US$0.097 (9.7 cents).

Example 3

We can also calculate pip values for the yen, but need to remember that any currency pair that involves the Japanese yen only involves two decimal places.

Solution

Buy USD/JPY at an exchange rate of 84.10.
　　0.01/84.10 = 0.0001189.
　　Multiply by the lot size to determine pip value in dollars.
　　For a standard lot US$0.0001189 × 100 000 = US$11.89.
　　For a mini lot US$0.0001189 × 10 000 = $1.19.
　　For a micro lot US$0.0001189 × 1000 = US$0.12 (12 cents).

Tip

Your online trading platform will calculate pip values for you but it is important to know how they are calculated and why pip values vary for each currency pair.

The bid/offer spread

All forex quotes include a two-way price—the bid and the ask. The bid or buy price is always shown on the left-hand side, and the ask or sell price is always displayed on the right-hand side. The ask price is also called the offer price.

The bid price is the price that the buyer is willing to pay to buy the base currency, and represents the price at which you can sell.

The ask or offer price is the price that the seller is willing to sell the base currency, and represents the price at which you can buy.

The price quotes of the bid and the offer will have two components: the big figure and the dealing price. The big figure refers to the whole dollar price of the quote, and the dealing price refers to the last two digits. The big figure is generally shown in smaller type, while the dealing price is shown in larger and/or more brightly displayed type. An example is shown in figure 5.1.

Figure 5.1: the big figure and dealing price

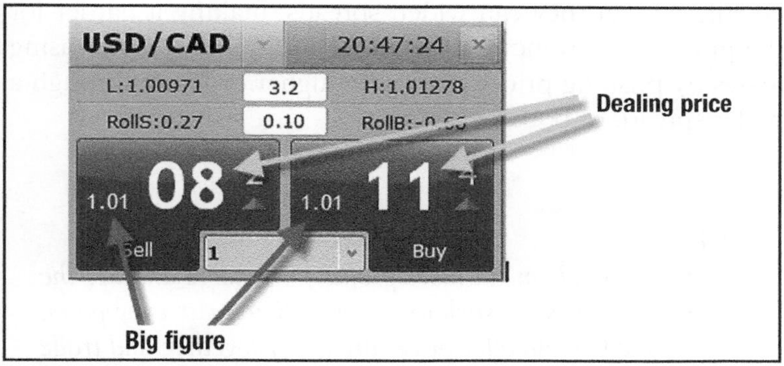

Source: FXCM Trading Station, <www.fxcm.com>.

In this example of the USD/CAD currency pair the big figure is 1.01, and the dealing price is 0.0008 bid/0.0011 offered. You can also see that the bid price or the price at which you can sell is 1.0108, and the ask or offer price at which you can buy is 1.0111.

The difference between the bid and the ask prices is referred to as the spread. The spread between the bid and the ask price in this example is 3 pips (1.0111 − 1.0108) and represents the cost of establishing, or opening, a position. From the outset of a trade, the trader must recover the cost of the spread before they make any profit. The spread also represents the minimum move required by the currency pair before the position is at break even for the trader. Looking at our example of the USD/CAD, if you decide to buy, you will pay 1.0111 and the pair currently has a 3 pip spread. In order for us to break even, or make no loss, on this trade, the offer price would have to move up to 1.0114, and the bid price would then move to 1.0111, assuming the spread remained at 3 pips. This is referred to as crossing the spread, and it is an unavoidable fact of life for spot forex traders.

Wider spreads result in higher ask and lower bid prices. The wider the spread, the more the price has to move in the trader's favour before they are in profit on a trade. Market makers make most of their profit through the price spread—you can now understand how. In a fast-moving or volatile market they can widen spreads, making it harder for the price of a currency pair to move into profit, or increasing losses by pushing prices artificially higher or lower through a wider spread, or both.

Tip

Tighter spreads mean more profits for traders and are the reasons it is wise to stick to the more liquid currency pairs, where the bid and offer prices are closer together, and trade with retail forex firms that maintain tight price spreads.

How the trader and the dealer can both make a profit

Since the object of trading is to make a profit and the dealing firms are also in business to generate a profit, we need to look at how both traders and dealing firms can make profits on the same transaction. A trader decides to buy one standard lot (100 000) of AUD/USD. The DMA or NDD firm platform shows a 3 pip spread of say 0.9657/0.9660, allowing the client to place an order to buy (go long) AUD/USD at 0.9659 through the online trading platform. The dealer relays the order through its back-end bridge or API to the banks and liquidity providers that it has credit relationships with, and it receives the following tradeable bid/offer prices:

Bank A: AUD/USD 0.9657/0.9658

Bank B: AUD/USD 0.9656/0.9657

Bank C: AUD/USD 0.9658/0.9659

The dealer confirms the trade to the client at the quoted price of 0.9660, representing 0.9659 (the price from Bank C) plus a 1 pip mark-up, or commission. The dealing firm then offsets the trade by buying from Bank B at 0.9657 (the lowest ask price, from Bank B). By offsetting the trade in the inter-bank market the firm is able to remain neutral as to whether the client makes or loses money on the trade.

The market moves in the trader's favour, and the dealing firm platform now shows AUD/USD at 0.9757/0.9760 (the best bid/ask price plus a 1 pip mark-up), and so the client closes the trade by selling at 0.9757 (the bid price). At the same time, the dealer sees the following tradeable bid/offer prices from its bank market makers:

Bank A: AUD/USD 0.9757/0.9758

Bank B: AUD/USD 0.9756/0.9757

Bank C: AUD/USD 0.9758/0.9759

The dealing firm closes its long position by selling in the inter-bank market at 0.9758 (the highest bid price from Bank C).

Let's check out the results for both the trader and the DMA or NDD firm.

The client opens the trade at 0.9660 and closes it out at 0.9757, for a gain of 97 pips. On one standard lot with a pip value of US$10 per pip, the client has made $970 profit (97 pips × $10 per pip).

The dealing firm opens the trade at 0.9657 and closes it out at 0.9758, for a gain of 101 pips, or $1010, plus a 1 pip mark-up on either side, or $20, making a gain of $1030. From this they have to pay the client the $970 profit, leaving $60.00, and fees to their prime broker and other parties, which may total $20, leaving a net profit of $40. Now multiply this by the thousands of trades being transacted every day! Bear in mind, however, that the dealing firm has other hidden costs, such as the provision of trading platforms, price streaming, and maintaining support desks, services supplied free of charge to the client.

Fractional pips

A recent development by some retail forex dealing firms has been the introduction of fractional pips, by adding another digit onto the currency pairs—either a fifth digit for most currencies or a third digit for pairs involving the Japanese yen. This is not a whole pip, but one that is one-tenth the value of a whole pip. Fractional pips have long been available in the inter-bank market.

Tip

The availability of fractional pips serves to narrow the spread between the bid and the ask.

Figure 5.2 shows a quote of EUR/USD with fractional pips.

Figure 5.2: EUR/USD with fractional pips quoted

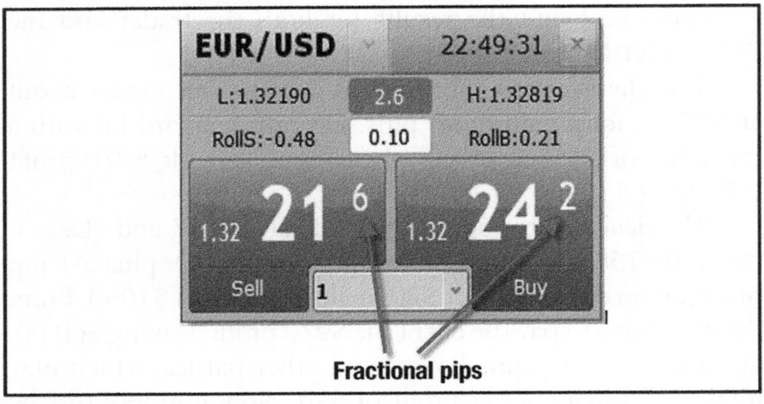

Fractional pips

Source: FXCM Trading Station, <www.fxcm.com>.

As you can see, the full pip bid is 1.3221, and the offer is 1.3224, or a 3 pip spread.

However, this platform also shows fractional pips that are one-tenth of a full pip. These are the '6' on the bid side and the '2' on the ask side. Once these are taken into consideration, the spread between the bid and ask is now 2.6 pips (1.3224 2/10 – 1.3221 6/10). The availability of fractional pips narrowed the spread by 0.4 of a full pip. On one standard lot of 100 000 this represents around US$4.

Tip

Remember not to count the fifth digit as a whole pip.

While fractional pips serve to narrow the bid/ask spread, remember not to count them as whole pips when calculating entry prices, stop losses and profit targets. If you forget and use them as whole pips you can be triggered in or out of a trade by mistake. For example, say you set a stop loss 50 pips under your long entry price. If you count the fifth digit (or third digit in a pair involving the yen) then you will have set your stop only 5 pips away from your entry point and you could get stopped out within a few seconds.

The same applies when setting a profit target. You may set a target 80 pips away from your entry price, but if you mistakenly calculate the price using the fractional pips, you will set the target only 8 pips away.

Tip

Don't use fractional pips when calculating stops or profit targets. Be aware that your platform uses them and that they benefit the spread, but focus only on the whole pips for your calculations.

Margin and leverage

When trading forex, we are trading using leverage. As the instruments have a minimum trade size in units of the base currency (1 standard lot = 100 000 units), the use of margin is necessary.

Tip

The concepts of leverage and margin work hand in hand, but both terms have very distinct meanings and it is important to understand both.

Leverage is the use of financial instruments or borrowed capital (such as a margin trading account) to increase the potential return of any investment. Put another way, leverage is the ability to control a large amount of money by using some of your own cash and borrowing the rest. Any financial product or instrument that allows you to control a larger position than would be possible if you were trading the underlying instrument using your own money involves the use of leverage, and is called a derivative. In this way, all derivatives, including spot forex, are leveraged as they allow the use of relatively small amounts of capital to control much larger face-value positions. As a result, a small movement in the price of the underlying instrument results in a much larger change in the value of the derivative.

Leverage can be thought of as a loan that is provided by the dealer or broker with whom your trading account is held. The money deposited into your trading account is used as a security deposit against the funds that you borrow to control much larger positions—in other words, we have been able to leverage up the cash in the account. Let's look at how leverage can work to increase both profits and losses in a trading situation.

You enter a trade buying one standard ($100 000) lot, and it increases in value to $102 000, giving you a profit of $2000. If you could only use leverage of 1:1 you would need to stump up the full $100 000 amount, and you would earn a return of 2 per cent on the trade. If, however, you were using leverage of 100:1 (effectively borrowing $100 000), for example, you would only need to contribute $1000 of your own cash to control the same $100 000 position. The return on your capital would now be 200 per cent ($2000 profit/$1000 of your capital used).

If, on the other hand, the position fell to $98 000, you have now lost $2000. If you had stumped up the full $100 000 (leverage of 1:1) you have a −2 per cent return, or 2 per cent loss. However, if you were trading on leverage of 100:1 using $1000 of your own money, your return would be −200 per cent ($2000 loss/$1000 capital).

Tip

You can now see why leverage is referred to as a double-edged sword.

Leverage can be defined as gaining assistance or advantage through the use of a tool or lever. The tool or lever in trading terms is the use of margin. Trading on margin means that you are able to enter into positions that are much larger than the balance of cash in your trading account. The cash held in your trading account serves as a safety deposit, or collateral, for the broker or dealer, from whom you then borrow the balance. Margin serves as collateral to cover any losses that may occur. Since nothing is actually being purchased or sold for delivery, only the promise to exchange the difference in cash between two prices, the only real purpose for having funds in an account with a dealer or provider is for sufficient margin to be available with which to trade, and to cover amounts lost in losing trades.

Leverage is often used to describe trading on margin, and is descriptive of margin trading requirements, as the two terms go hand in hand. A leverage of 100:1, for example, implies a margin requirement of 1 per cent. In other words, if you wish to open a position using a leverage of 100:1 you are required to have 1 per cent of the size of the position available as cash in your margin trading account. As an example, to open a position with a face value of $100000 (one standard lot), using leverage of 100:1 would require a 1 per cent margin, or $1000. To open a position with a face value of $10000 (one mini lot), using leverage of 100:1 would require a 1 per cent margin or $100. A leverage of 50:1 implies a margin requirement of 2 per cent. To open one standard lot using a leverage of 50:1 would require a margin of $2000. A leverage of 200:1 implies a margin requirement of 0.5 per cent, meaning a standard lot could be opened with a margin of $500.

Tip

Margin requirements and the leverage available will vary from broker to broker.

Based on the margin required you can calculate the maximum leverage available to you as shown in table 5.5.

Table 5.5: margin and maximum leverage levels

Margin requirement	Maximum leverage
5%	20:1
3%	33:1
2%	50:1
1%	100:1
0.50%	200:1
0.25%	400:1

One of the attractions of the spot forex market to many traders is the availability of high leverage levels and the use of margin. Without these, trading forex would be beyond the reach of the vast majority of retail traders, who would be unable to place trades in lots of $100 000 with a 1:1 leverage. The availability of leverage and the use of margin allow small traders access to the market.

Tip

Without the use of leverage and margin, retail forex trading would not be financially viable because massive moves in currency prices would be needed in order to generate profits.

The use of a margin trading account means, for example, that we can technically control $100 000 worth of a currency pair, using a leverage of 100:1 and a margin requirement of 1 per cent, with $1000 of our own cash. As we know from the earlier examples, the value of 1 pip on one standard $100 000 lot is worth around $10. If the value of the currency pair rises by 50 pips, we have now made $500. Without the use of margin, if we could only purchase $1000 worth of the currency pair, the same 50 pip move would return a $5 profit. To make the same $500 profit without the use of leverage and margin would require a 5000 pip move.

Misunderstanding and misusing leverage and margin is the key reason many retail forex traders lose money and blow up their trading accounts when trading forex. We will take a detailed look into ways to appropriately manage the risks involved in forex trading using leverage and margin in chapter 9.

Tip

Just because the broker offers the ability to trade with 200:1 leverage doesn't mean you have to do it. The amount of leverage you use will depend on your broker and what you feel comfortable with.

When to trade forex

While the forex market is open 24 hours per day for five and a half days per week, from its open early Monday morning in New Zealand to the close of the New York session in the early hours of Saturday morning Sydney time, the market is not always active and some times are better than others to trade, when activity, and so intra-day liquidity, is higher. This is particularly relevant for short-term intra-day traders who need high levels of market activity and volatility to generate the price fluctuations they need when attempting to make lots of trades for small profits. It is less important for more medium-term traders, who are keying their decisions to buy and sell off end-of-day prices.

Tip

Although the spot forex market is referred to as operating 24 hours a day, there is actually a brief period between the close of the New York session and the beginning of the New Zealand session. End-of-day traders and trading systems use these times as the open and close for each day's trading session.

The largest amount of trading volume in forex occurs during the London session, followed by the New York session and then the Tokyo session. During the times when these centres are trading, activity is at its highest. These are the important times for short-term traders, and unfortunately for those of us in Australia and New Zealand the really active trading during the London and New York sessions occurs during our night-time. Table 5.6 shows the approximate opening and closing times for each of the major sessions as the forex market follows the sun around the globe.

Table 5.6: forex session trading times for Sydney, Tokyo, London and New York

Time zone	GMT	US EST	Sydney Time
Sydney open	22.00	17.00	08.00
Sydney close	07.00	02.00	18.00
Tokyo open	0.00	19.00	10.00
Tokyo close	09.00	03.00	20.00
London open	08.00	05.00	19.00
London close	17.00	12.00	03.00
New York open	13.00	08.00	23.00
New York close	22.00	17.00	07.00

These times may be approximate due to the effects of daylight saving at different times of the year in different time zones. The market does open in New Zealand a few hours before the Sydney open, but activity tends to be light until Sydney gets started.

Tip

The really high levels of activity and volatility tend to occur when two trading sessions are open at the same time, particularly when London and New York are open together.

The cross-over times, when forex markets are open together, are shown in table 5.7.

Table 5.7: overlapping trading sessions for the forex market

GMT	6	7	8	9	10	11	12	13	14	15	16	17	18	19	20	21	22	23	24	1	2	3	4	5
Sydney	17	18	19	20	21	22	23	24	1	2	3	4	5	6	7	8	9	10	11	12	13	14	15	16
US EST	1	2	3	4	5	6	7	8	9	10	11	12	13	14	15	16	17	18	19	20	21	22	23	24

The shaded session bars show:
- **LONDON** (beginning around GMT 8 through GMT 17)
- **NEW YORK** (beginning around GMT 13 through GMT 22)
- **SYDNEY** (beginning around GMT 22 through GMT 7)
- **TOKYO** (beginning around GMT 24 through GMT 9)

Tip

The times when both New York and London are open together is referred to as the NYLON.

Though trading activity is at its highest during the London and New York sessions, activity does build up through the Sydney session, and when Tokyo and Sydney are open simultaneously. This is particularly so in the local currencies for these two trading sessions—Aussie dollar crosses and yen crosses.

Chapter summary

⇨ Buying a currency is like buying a share in a particular country.

⇨ Until the late 1990s, only the big guys could participate in forex trading. The initial requirement was a trading account in excess of $US10 million.

⇨ The exchange rate of a currency is its relative value compared with the price of another currency.

⇨ Currencies are always quoted in pairs. The first currency in the pair is known as the base currency. The second currency in the pair is called the quote currency or sometimes the counter currency.

⇨ The most actively traded currency pairs are referred to as the majors and generally involve the US dollar on one side of the deal. Any currency pair that does not involve the US dollar is referred to as a cross currency pair, cross rate or cross.

⇨ Cross rates are derived from the respective US dollar–related pairs but are quoted independently.

⇨ A pip is the smallest incremental price move of a currency pair. Pip stands for percentage in point or price interest point.

⇨ Currencies are traded in lots—standard lots of 100 000, mini lots of 10 000, and micro lots of 1000.

⇨ All forex quotes include a two-way price—the bid and the ask. The bid or buy price is always displayed on the left-hand side, and the ask or sell price is always displayed on the right-hand side. The ask price is also called the offer price.

⇨ Wider spreads result in higher ask and lower bid prices. The wider the spread, the more the price has to move in the trader's favour before they are in profit on a trade.

⇨ A recent development by some retail forex dealing firms has been the introduction of fractional pips.

⇨ Leverage is the use of financial instruments or borrowed capital (such as a margin trading account) to increase the potential return of any investment.

⇨ Trading on margin means that you are able to enter into positions that are much larger than the balance of cash in your trading account.

⇨ The forex market is open 24 hours a day for five and a half days per week, from its open early Monday morning, Sydney time, in New Zealand to the close of the New York session in the early hours of Saturday morning Sydney time.

chapter 6

How to place a forex trade

Now that we have discussed in detail the workings of the spot forex market and the important concepts of currency pairs, pips, lot sizes, bid/ask spreads, the best times to trade forex and the use of leverage and margin, it is now time to look at the process of actually placing trades on a forex trading platform. In this chapter we will work through the process of placing a trade at market, as well as the use of stop and limit orders. We will also take a look at the process of rollover and the use of carry trades to profit from interest rate differences between currency pairs.

Placing a trade

Having chosen your preferred retail forex dealer and opened and funded your margin trading account, now comes time to place trades. Your trading decisions to buy and sell will be based on fundamental or technical analysis techniques that are beyond the scope of this book. Your position sizing and money management rules will be dictated by your account size, appetite for risk, and risk management, which are discussed in chapter 9. For the sake of simplicity and ease of operation, let's assume that you have opened an account with $15000 and you are able to trade mini lots (10000) on this account.

Opening a trade at market

Opening a trade at market, or at best, means you are willing to deal immediately at the prevailing bid or offer. If you want to buy at market, you take the prevailing ask or offer price (the price the seller is offering and thus the price at which we must buy). This is referred to as hitting the offer. If you want to sell at market, you take the prevailing bid or buy price (the price the buyer is willing to pay and thus the price at which we must sell). This is referred to as hitting the bid.

In the example shown in figure 6.1 of the AUD/USD currency pair, you can see that the bid (the price at which we can sell at market) is 0.9851 $^2\!/_{10}$ and the ask (the price at which we can buy at market) is 0.9854 $^0\!/_{10}$.

Figure 6.1: AUD/USD bid/ask

Source: FXCM Trading Station, <www.fxcm.com>.

In order to buy at market, or hit the offer, simply click on the buy side and the window shown in figure 6.2 appears.

Figure 6.2: buying at best, or at market

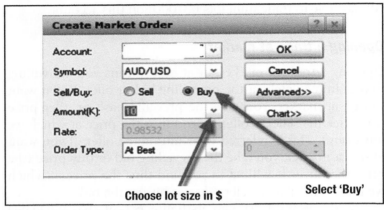

Source: FXCM Trading Station, <www.fxcm.com>.

You can clearly see that we have selected to buy one mini lot ($10 000) of AUD/USD. To execute the order simply click on the OK button and the order is sent to market, and the order will be filled at the offer price.

If we were selling to open a short position at best, we would follow the same process, but clicking on *sell* rather than buy.

Using stop and limit orders to enter a trade

At best orders are used to enter a trade immediately, but stop and limit orders can be used to enter trades above or below the prevailing market price. Stop and limit entry orders will be used more by end-of-day and medium-term traders, who are waiting for some price- or momentum-based confirmation before entering a trade.

On the buy side, stop orders can be used to enter a trade above the prevailing price, and limit orders will be used to enter a trade below the prevailing market price.

On the short or sell side, stop orders will be used to enter a trade below the prevailing market price, and limit orders will be used to enter a trade above the prevailing market price.

The way to enter an order on stop or limit will vary from platform to platform, so the following process may differ depending on the platform being used. Some platforms will require that you enter the order as a stop or a limit by selecting one of these options from a drop-down menu; others will recognise automatically that the order is either a stop or limit order depending on the price the trader sets in their order to open the trade compared with the prevailing market price. The example shown in figure 6.3 is from such a platform.

Let's work through an example of buying long on a stop (above the prevailing market price) using the EUR/USD currency pair. Figure 6.3 shows the bid and offer prices being displayed on the platform for the EUR/USD currency pair.

Figure 6.3: bid/ask spread for EUR/USD

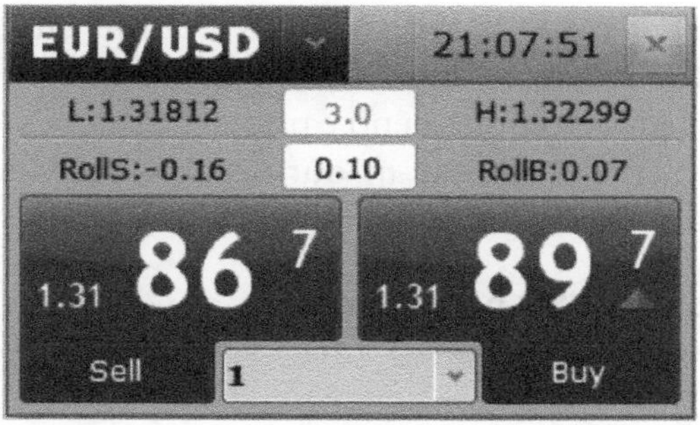

Source: FXCM Trading Station, <www.fxcm.com>.

Let's assume you want to buy EUR/USD at 1.3195 (ignoring fractional pips), which is above the present offer price of 1.3189 (ignoring fractional pips). You are buying on stop as your buy price is above the current market price, and you don't want to enter this trade until you have confirmation that the price is moving higher.

The next step is to right-click on the bid/ask window; the window shown in figure 6.4 will appear.

Figure 6.4: buying EUR/USD on stop

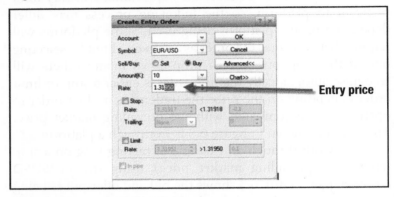

Source: FXCM Trading Station, <www.fxcm.com>.

In this window, select the rate at which you want your entry order to be executed; in this example of EUR/USD, it is 1.3195. We then click on the OK button, and the order is sent to the dealer to await execution when or if the price reaches our predetermined entry price.

The order will appear in our account as a pending or waiting order, as shown in figure 6.5.

Figure 6.5: EUR/USD pending order

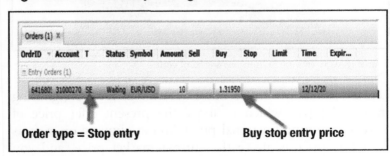

Source: FXCM Trading Station, <www.fxcm.com>.

The same process is followed to enter a buy limit entry order, and stop and limit short-sell entry orders.

You can also enter any predetermined stop loss and profit target prices you have for a trade.

Tip

A stop loss determines the price at which you will exit a trade that has moved against you to a price level that corresponds with the maximum amount of capital you are prepared to lose on any one trade. All trades must be entered with a predetermined stop-loss level set.

Tip

A profit target is a predetermined price at which we will exit a profitable trade.

Using the EUR/USD example, you have now set the price at which you want to enter the trade. At the same time you can enter the stop loss and the profit targets for this trade. For this example, let's assume you want to set a stop loss 50 pips below the entry price and a profit target 100 pips above the entry price.

Your on stop entry price is set at 1.3195. The stop loss is 1.3195 − 50 pips = 1.3145. The profit target is 1.3195 + 100 pips = 1.3295. We now enter these as shown in figure 6.6.

When you click on the OK button, the whole order is sent to the dealer. The on stop entry order now has both a stop loss and a profit target order attached to it as shown in figure 6.7. Neither of these will be activated until the original buy stop order is filled. All legs or sides of the order can be cancelled or changed at any time.

Figure 6.6: stop loss and profit target for EUR/USD

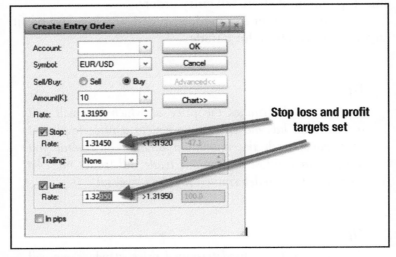

Source: FXCM Trading Station, <www.fxcm.com>.

Figure 6.7: EUR/USD with all three legs

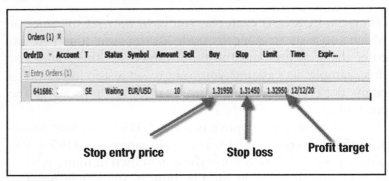

Source: FXCM Trading Station, <www.fxcm.com>.

The same process is followed to set up short sell entry orders with stop losses set above the entry price and profit targets set below the entry price. The above examples show the platform functionality of the Trading Station platform of forex trading firm FXCM.

Tip

Trading platforms will vary in how you enter and set orders. It is very important to familiarise yourself with the operation of the platform you are using and how to enter the various order types.

Rollover

Rollover is a way of extending the settlement date of an open spot forex position. Usually in spot forex currency trades, you must take delivery of the currency and deliver the currency you have borrowed or sold two days after the transaction date. By simultaneously closing out of the existing position (by selling the bought, or long, side of the trade and buying back the sold, or short, side of the trade) at that day's closing price and re-entering at the opening price the following day, you have rolled the position over to the next day and added another day to the settlement date. This rollover process can be continued for an indefinite period until you decide to close or exit the open position when a profit price is reached or you close the position at a loss. Your forex dealing firm, acting on your behalf, automatically executes the rollover process in your account.

Tip

If you hold a spot forex position overnight—that is, the position is rolled over—then you may pay or receive what is called the rollover fee.

For most forex traders, who aim to make a profit from the changes in exchange rates rather than actually taking delivery of the currency, rollover (which is often referred to as tomorrow next) is useful because it allows trades to be held open indefinitely, as the open position can be continually rolled over until such time as the trade is finally closed. Every currency trade involves borrowing one currency to buy another, so when you roll over an open position, rollover charges come into play. You may have to pay interest on the currency that is borrowed, and may receive the interest earned on the one that is bought. If you buy a currency pair where the base currency has a *higher* inter-bank interest rate than the quote currency, then you will receive interest, or a rollover fee; if the base currency has a *lower* interest rate than the quote currency, you will have to pay interest, or a rollover fee. For example, if you buy the AUD/USD, and the inter-bank interest rates are higher in Australia than in the US, then you may receive a rollover fee (interest may be credited to your account). On the other hand, if the interest rates are higher in the US, then you may have to pay a rollover fee (interest charges will be debited from your account).

Rollover fees do not affect day traders who close their positions at the end of each trading day. Rollovers only apply to any overnight open position carried over to the next day. Rollovers fees are applied to open positions after 5 pm EST in the US, after the close of the New York trading session.

The carry trade

The availability of the rollover function gives rise to the most popular trade in the forex market—the carry trade. It is a trading strategy employed by the large hedge funds and fund managers, but smaller traders can use it just as easily, albeit on a smaller scale.

The carry trade revolves around the fact that every currency's value relative to another's is closely related to the interest rates in the two countries involved. The idea behind the carry trade is to make use of these differences in interest rates to earn a profit by buying (going long) a currency with a high interest rate and selling (going short) a currency with a low interest rate.

Tip

The carry trade uses the fact that when we are trading forex we are actually borrowing the currency we are selling to finance the purchase of the currency we are buying.

The basis of the carry trade is to go long a currency pair where there is a large difference in interest rates, so that the interest earned on the long currency more than covers the interest you have to pay on the short, or borrowed currency. Even without any beneficial movement in the price of the pair, the interest earned can be quite substantial because of the use of leverage. If we use one standard lot of $100 000 as an example, and the NZD/JPY currency pair where the interest rate differential has been as high as 7.25 per cent, we can do some maths to help understand the workings of the carry trade and the benefits of the use of leverage in using this strategy.

Without the use of leverage, a $100 000 position at a 1:1 leverage would have earned a 7.25 per cent return or around $7250. If we assume that this trade could have been entered with the use of 100:1 leverage, or a 1 per cent margin requirement, then the same $100 000 position only requires the use of $1000 of available trading capital. Since the carry applies to the face value of the position, we have still earned $7250, but have only used $1000 of our capital as margin for the trade—a 725 per cent annual return! You can now

130

see why the carry trade is a popular trade. If you add the fact that the value of the pair may also increase in value, then the returns can be better still. Figure 6.8 shows the rise in value of the NZD/JPY pair between 2002 and 2007, as the interest rate differential increased from just under 5 per cent to more than 7 per cent as the Reserve Bank of New Zealand raised rates, and interest rates in Japan remained at 0.0 per cent.

Figure 6.8: NZD/JPY carry trade example, 2002 to 2007

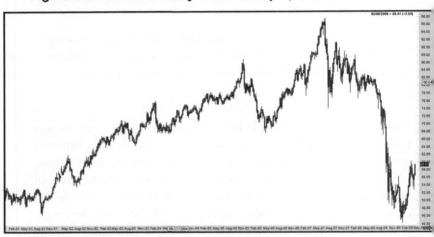

Source: Trade Navigator © Genesis Financial Technologies, Inc.

What is also evident from this chart is that, like all trades, you still need a point at which you will exit the trade when it starts to move against you. Despite the difference in interest rates and the returns that could be earned from this carry trade, when everything turned sour during the global financial crisis in 2008, even the high-yielding carry trades were unwound as traders and investors bailed out of high-yielding and perceived high-risk currencies such as the New Zealand dollar, and sought solace in cash or safe-haven currencies like the US dollar, Japanese yen and Swiss franc. When carry trades are unwound, the declines can be swift and severe, as in the previous example, as everyone runs for the exit at the same time. The profits from the carry are not enough to offset the capital losses, so the carry trades are liquidated.

Tip

Carry trades can be a great way to profit from interest rate differentials, but you must still know when to exit the trade.

Chapter summary

⇨ Opening a trade at market, or at best, means you are willing to deal immediately at the prevailing bid or offer.

⇨ On the buy side, stop orders can be used to enter a trade above the prevailing price, and limit orders will be used to enter a trade below the prevailing market price.

⇨ On the short, or sell, side, stop orders will be used to enter a trade below the prevailing market price, and limit orders will be used to enter a trade above the prevailing market price.

⇨ Various combinations of stop and limit orders can be used to enter and exit trades depending on your trading style or the trading system or strategy being used.

⇨ Rollover in forex trading is a way of extending the settlement date of an open position.

⇨ The availability of rollover gives rise to the most popular trade in the forex market — the carry trade. It is a trading strategy employed by the large hedge funds and fund managers, but smaller traders can also use it, albeit on a smaller scale, to benefit from differences between the interest rates in the countries whose currencies they are trading.

chapter 7

Currency futures

The primary reason for the existence of the foreign exchange market is to facilitate the exchange of one currency for another to assist international trade. Over time the forex market has developed as an efficient means for buyers and sellers who hold different currencies, and who have different views on the relative values of currencies, to find each other and conduct trades. This has seen a massive increase in speculative trades in order to generate profits from the movements in currency exchange rates. A number of instruments are available to market participants, whether hedgers or speculators, who want to trade forex. The two main instruments available to retail forex traders are the spot forex market, as discussed in detail in chapter 5, and currency futures.

Currency futures have been available since their introduction by the Chicago Mercantile Exchange (CME) in 1972, and their use by traders has been steadily increasing over the years. While much of the discussion, marketing and promotional activities surrounding the trading of forex have to deal with the spot forex market, trading currency futures is also a great way to participate in the forex market. For existing futures traders, currency futures are another contract they can successfully trade.

Tip

For new and potential traders getting started in the forex market, currency futures need to be fully considered and understood as a viable alternative to trading spot forex.

Currency futures, and how they compare with spot forex, are the subjects of this chapter. We will also be looking at trading currency futures on the CME, as the CME is the largest regulated market for trading currency futures: it had a daily turnover in 2009 of more than US$100 billion.

The mechanics of trading currency futures

Like spot forex, currency futures express the value of one currency relative to the value of another or the value of the exchange rate between the two currencies. As with the spot forex market, currency futures are also always quoted in pairs, and the same terminology applies. The first currency in the pair is known as the base currency. It is the currency you are buying or selling and is the basis for the transaction. The second currency in the pair is called the quote currency or sometimes the counter currency.

Price quotes are often referred to as being either European- or American-style quotes and are based on historical trading conventions that have become internationally accepted standards. These terms reflect the position of the US dollar in the currency pair. European-style quotes express the amount of currency that can be exchanged for US$1. The US dollar is quoted first and is the base currency. European-style quotes for forex pairs are only used in spot forex. American-style quotes express the amount of US dollars needed for one unit of the foreign currency. The US dollar is quoted second and is the quote or counter currency. American-style quotes are always quoted in US dollars and cents.

Tip

Just as with spot forex, the exchange rate in currency futures is the price of the base currency in terms of, or relative to, the quote currency. If, for example, the EUR/USD pair is quoted at 1.3695, this means that 1 euro can buy 1.3695 US dollars, or that it takes 1.3695 US dollars to buy 1 euro.

Major futures contracts traded on the CME are quoted in American style. Table 7.1 (overleaf) lists the major currency pairs available as futures contracts on the CME; these are often referred to as the G10 currency pairs because they contain the currencies of the G10 countries. They may be standard pairs that contain the US dollar, or currency crosses, or cross rates that do not contain the US dollar. Cross rates do not contain the US dollar, and express the value of the base currency in terms of the quote currency. The EUR/GBP cross rate, for example, reflects how many British pounds you can buy for 1 euro.

Aside from their use by traders and speculators, cross rates are important for companies and other entities trading in global markets, but who don't need exchange rates involving the US dollar. A manufacturer located in Japan that is exporting to a wholesaler in France is more interested in the relative value of the yen to the euro (EUR/JPY cross rate) than the yen to the US dollar (USD/JPY).

Table 7.1: major currency futures pairs on CME

AUD/USD	EUR/CAD
AUD/CAD	EUR/CHF
AUD/JPY	EUR/JPY
AUD/NZD	EUR/NOK
CAD/USD	EUR/SEK
CAD/JPY	GBP/USD
CHF/USD	GBP/JPY
CHF/JPY	GBP/CHF
Dow Jones CME FX$INDEX	JPY/USD
EUR/USD	E-mini JPY/USD
E-mini EUR/USD	NOK/USD
EUR/AUD	NZD/USD
EUR/GBP	SEK/USD

Source: CME Group.

In addition to the currency futures contracts available on the G10 currency pairs, futures contracts are also available on many exotic pairs or currency cross rates. These currency futures have been developed by the CME to allow traders to gain access to exchange rate markets that they are otherwise unable to trade, such as the Chinese yuan, Korean won, and many others. Table 7.2 is a list of the currency futures contracts available on these currency pairs. They are referred to as emerging market currency pairs.

Tip

An economy in the process of industrialisation, and thus having only a short association with global financial markets, is referred to as an emerging market.

Emerging market countries are often subject to more geo-political, economic and social risk than the more economically developed countries. As a result, higher volatility and potential risk are often associated with the currencies of these emerging market countries.

Table 7.2: emerging market currency pairs on CME

BRL/USD	PLN/EUR
CZK/USD	RMB/USD
CZK/EUR	RMB/EUR
HUF/EUR	RMB/JPY
HUF/USD	RUB/USD
ILS/USD	ZAR/USD
KRW/USD	USD/TRY
MXN/USD	EUR/TRY
PLN/USD	

Source: CME Group.

Tip

When trading the emerging markets contracts liquidity will be much less than when trading the major currency futures contracts. Bid/ask spreads may also be wider.

The largest of these emerging market economies are Brazil, Russia, India and China. They are often referred to as the BRIC economies or BRIC countries—Brazil is the largest of the Latin American economies, Russia is still the dominant economy in eastern Europe, India is the second-largest economy in Asia, with a burgeoning middle class, and China has the largest economy in Asia and is rapidly becoming a leading world economy. The BRIC currencies are the Brazilian real, Russian rouble (or ruble), Indian rupee and Chinese yuan.

Long or short?

Currency futures can be traded long or short with the same ease as in spot forex. Going long (buying) and going short

(short selling) are the two major futures trading strategies. Traders and speculators are able to take a long or short position depending on their view of the market and their expectations of future price moves.

If, for example, you expect the price of the Aussie dollar to increase you would buy, or go long, an Australian dollar currency futures contract and close out of the position for a profit when the price rises—benefiting from the rise in price. If, on the other hand, you expect a decline in the value of the Aussie dollar you can sell, or go short, an Australian dollar currency futures contract and buy it back again for a profit when the prices falls—benefiting from the decline in the price.

Tip

The forex markets provide ample opportunities for trading both long and short, so it is important to understand the two concepts and be able to trade both sides of the market or price trend.

Because futures contracts are exchangeable between parties before the settlement or expiry date, traders and speculators are able to buy and sell contracts to profit from the price fluctuations that are occurring constantly. This ability to eliminate an open position by buying or selling the opposite position is known as offsetting. If you are short a Canadian dollar contract, for example, you simply buy back a Canadian dollar contract and your trading account is either credited if you have made a profit, or debited if you have incurred a loss. If you are long and wish to close out the trade, you simply sell.

Novation

In order to handle the constant transfer of futures contracts between buyers and sellers, futures exchanges have developed clearing operations that record all transactions and document the transfer of contracts between the parties involved. This clearing operation assumes the role of a third party to every transaction in a matching process called novation. In this process the clearing house assumes the role of buyer against the original buyer and seller against the original seller. It operates as though the seller has sold to the clearing house and the buyer has bought from the clearing house to ensure the integrity of every trade.

By placing itself between the two counterparties to every trade, the clearing house guarantees that each trade will be honoured and settled as set out in the futures contract, and so buyers and sellers do not deal directly with each other, avoiding exposure to credit and counterparty default risk. This novation process can be used because the number of long contracts is always equal to the number of short contracts, and the clearing house is continually matching buyers with sellers through the regulated exchange process. It ensures a default-free trading environment for all traders.

Tip

The result of the actions of the clearing house is that futures contracts never exist directly between a buyer and a seller — each client has a contract with the clearing house, greatly reducing the risks of traders dealing directly with unknown parties.

Standardised contracts and specifications

Unlike the decentralised OTC spot forex market, currency futures are traded on a regulated exchange, such as the CME and others that provide rules and regulations for trading in these financial products. As a result, currency futures contracts, like all futures contracts, have standard specifications—contract size, expiry or delivery date, and minimum price increment and corresponding value. This means that all the features of the contract are the same to each buyer and seller; the only variable is price, and price rises and falls in line with supply and demand.

Figure 7.1 shows the features of a standardised AUD/USD currency futures contract, which we will discuss in detail.

Figure 7.1: Aussie dollar futures contract specifications

Contract Size	100,000 Australian dollars
Contract Month Listings	Six months in the March quarterly cycle (Mar, Jun, Sep, Dec)
Settlement Procedure	Physical Delivery
Position Accountability	6,000 contracts
Ticker Symbol	CME Globex Electronic Markets: 6A Open Outcry: AD AON Code: LA View product and vendor codes
Minimum Price Increment	$.0001 per Australian dollar increments ($10.00/contract). $.00005 per Australian dollar increments ($5.00/contract) for AUD/USD futures intra-currency spreads executed on the trading floor and electronically, and for AON transactions.
Trading Hours	**OPEN OUTCRY (RTH):** 7:20 a.m.–2:00 p.m. **GLOBEX (ETH):** Sundays: 5:00 p.m. – 4:00 p.m. Central Time (CT) next day. Monday – Friday: 5:00 p.m. – 4:00 p.m. CT the next day, except on Friday - closes at 4:00 p.m. and reopens Sunday at 5:00 p.m. CT. **CME ClearPort:** Sunday – Friday 6:00 p.m. – 5:15 p.m. (5:00 p.m. – 4:15 p.m. Chicago Time/CT) with a 45-minute break each day beginning at 5:15 p.m. (4:15 p.m. CT)
Last Trade Date / Time View calendar	9:16 a.m. Central Time (CT) on the second business day immediately preceding the third Wednesday of the contract month (usually Monday).
Exchange Rule	These contracts are listed with, and subject to, the rules and regulations of CME.
Block Trade Eligibility	Yes. View more on Block Trade eligible contracts.
Block Trade Minimum	100 contracts
EFP Eligibility	Yes. View more on EFPs.

Source: CME Group.

Delivery (or maturity) date

All futures contracts have a defined expiry date, when they must be either delivered or settled in cash depending on the terms of the contract. The delivery dates for currency futures are typically the third Wednesday of March, June, September and December. The last trading day—the last day on which the contracts can be bought or sold before delivery day—is generally two days before. Most currency futures contracts are closed out before the last trading day with traders taking profits or cutting their losses, avoiding the need for cash or delivery settlement.

Settlement

Currency futures contracts can be settled in one of two ways. Most are offset by both buyers and sellers taking an opposite position to their current open position before the last trading day: a trader with an open long position will sell an equal number of contracts to close their open position; a trader with an open short position will buy back an equal number of contracts to close their open position. A profit is then credited to the trader's account, or a loss is debited from the trader's account.

Far less frequently, contracts are held until the maturity date. Contracts held until expiry must be either cash settled or physically delivered depending on the terms of the contract. Standard currency futures are subject to physical delivery, which means that the holder of a long position at the maturity date will receive the specified amount of the currency, while the holder of an open short position at the maturity date must deliver the specified amount of currency. This process is facilitated through the relevant futures exchange clearing house and the novation process, and payments are not made directly between the buyer and the seller. The clearing house collects the currency that must be delivered from the seller (the trader with the open short position), and will deliver it to the buyer (the trader with the open long position).

Contract size

Currency futures have a standard contract size expressed in the base currency. As shown in figure 7.1, the Australian dollar futures contract is for 100 000 Australian dollars. This is often referred to as the face value of the contract. The contract sizes for the other standard currency futures contracts are shown in table 7.3.

Table 7.3: standard futures contract sizes for the six major trading currencies

Currency	Standard contract size
Euro	125 000
British pounds	62 500
Japanese yen	12 500 000
Swiss francs	125 000
Canadian dollars	100 000
New Zealand dollars	100 000

Understanding tick values

Futures contracts also indicate the minimum price increment, giving rise to the tick value, or the smallest value by which the value of the contracts can change. The Aussie dollar contract above shows a minimum price increment of 0.0001, and a corresponding tick value of $10 ($100 000 face value × 0.0001 = $10).

As an example, if an Aussie dollar trade is entered long at 0.9867, the minimum next price it can move up to is 0.9868 (0.9867 + 0.0001 = 0.9868) and the minimum next price it can move down to is 0.9866 (0.9867 − 0.0001 = 0.9866). This 0.0001 point move is worth $10 per contract. If the price moves up from 0.9867 to 0.9887, this is a 0.0020 point move, called a 20 point move, representing a move of $200 per contract (20 points × $10 per point = $200). If the price moves up from 0.9867 to 0.9967, this is a 0.0100 point move, called a 100 point move, and represents a move of $1000 per contract (100 points × $10 per point = $1000).

Table 7.4 shows the contract size, minimum price increments and tick values for the more actively traded and liquid currency futures contracts.

Table 7.4: currency futures details

Futures contract	Currency pairs	Contract size	Minimum price increment	Tick value
Australian dollar	AUD/USD	100000 Australian dollars	0.0001	$10.00
Euro	EUR/USD	125000 euro	0.0001	$12.50
Swiss franc	CHF/USD	125000 Swiss francs	0.0001	$12.50
Japanese yen	JPY/USD	12500 Japanese yen	0.000001	$12.50
Canadian dollar	CAD/USD	100000 Canadian dollars	0.0001	$10.00
British pound	GBP/USD	62500 British pounds	0.0001	$6.25
NZ dollars	NZD/USD	100000 NZ dollars	0.0001	$10.00
Euro/pound	EUR/GBP	125000 euro	0.00005	£6.25
Euro/yen	EUR/JPY	125000 euro	0.01	¥1,250
Euro/Swiss	EUR/CHF	125000 euro	0.0001	Fr.12.50

E-micro currency futures

E-micro forex futures were introduced in March 2009 in recognition that standard currency futures contracts may be too large, in both size and margin requirement, for small retail traders, and to compete with the flexibility smaller traders have in trading mini and micro lots on the spot forex market. E-micro contracts are roughly one-tenth the size of the standard currency futures contracts. Figure 7.2 shows the e-micro contract for the Australian dollar, clearly showing the one-tenth difference in the size of the contract.

Figure 7.2: e-micro Australian dollar contract

Contract Size	10,000 Australian dollars
Contract Month Listings	Two months in the March quarterly cycle (Mar, Jun, Sep, Dec)
Settlement Procedure	Physically Delivered*
Position Accountability	60,000 E-micro contracts
Ticker Symbol	M6A View product and vendor codes
Minimum Price Fluctuation (Tick)	0.0001 USD/AUD (=US$1.00)
Contract Value	If USD/AUD = 0.6600 then contract = US$6,600 (= 10,000 AUD x US$0.6600/AUD)
Trading Hours	GLOBEX (ETH): Sundays: 5:00 p.m. – 4:00 p.m. Central Time (CT) next day. Monday – Friday: 5:00 p.m. – 4:00 p.m. CT the next day, except on Friday - closes at 4:00 p.m. and reopens Sunday at 5:00 p.m. CT. CME ClearPort: Sunday – Friday 6:00 p.m. – 5:15 p.m. (5:00 p.m. – 4:15 p.m. Chicago Time/CT) with a 45–minute break each day beginning at 5:15 p.m. (4:15 p.m. CT)
Last Trade Date / Time View calendar	9:16 a.m. Central Time (CT) on the second business day immediately preceding the third Wednesday of the contract month (usually Monday).
Exchange Rule	These contracts are listed with, and subject to, the rules and regulations of CME.
Block Trade Eligibility	No.
EFP Eligibility	Yes. View more on EFPs.
	*The September (U) 2010 E-micro Forex futures contracts are cash settled. However, starting with the December (Z) 2010 contract, CME FX will be migrating the E-micro Forex futures contracts from being cash settled to physically delivered. This will enable active traders to carry larger positions in the E-micros and easily offset them with our standard size FX contracts – potentially generating more liquidity and tighter spreads in the E-micro Forex futures contracts.

Source: CME Group.

The e-micro futures contracts available in late 2010 and their tick values are shown in table 7.5.

Table 7.5: e-micro contract sizes, minimum price increments and tick values available in late 2010

E-micro contract	Currency pair	Contract size	Minimum price increment	Tick value
Australian dollar	AUD/USD	10 000 Australian dollars	0.0001	$1.000
Euro	EUR/USD	12 500 euro	0.0001	$1.250
British pound	GBP/USD	6250 pounds	0.0001	$0.625
Swiss franc	CHF/USD	12 500 Swiss francs	0.0001	$1.250
Japanese yen	JPY/USD	1 250 000 Japanese yen	0.000001	$1.250
Canadian dollar	CAD/USD	10 000 Canadian dollars	0.0001	$1.000
US dollar/Yen	USD/JPY	10 000 US dollars	0.01	¥100
US dollar/Swiss franc	USD/CHF	10 000 US dollars	0.0001	Fr 1.00
US dollar/CAD	USD/CAD	10 000 US dollars	0.0001	CAD$1.00

The Aussie dollar e-micro contract represented in table 7.5 has a minimum price increment of 0.0001, and a corresponding tick value of $1 ($10 000 face value × 0.0001 = $10). As an example, if an Aussie dollar trade is entered long (buy) at 0.9867, the minimum next price it can move up to is 0.9868 (0.9867 + 0.0001 = 0.9868) and the minimum next price it can move down to is 0.9866 (0.9867 − 0.0001 = 0.9866). This 0.0001 point move is worth $1 per contract. If the price moves up from 0.9867 to 0.9887, this is a 0.0020 point move, called a 20 point move, and represents a move of $20 per contract (20 points × $10 per point = $20). If the price moves up from 0.9867 to 0.9967, this is a 0.0100 point move, called a 100 point move, and represents a move of $100 per contract (100 points × $1 per point = $100).

Tip

E-micro contracts can be used by traders wanting to trade smaller lot sizes on a regulated exchange rather than the unregulated over-the-counter spot forex market.

Bid/ask spread

All forex quotes include a two-way price—the bid and the ask. The bid or buy price is always displayed on the left-hand side, and the ask or sell price is always displayed on the-right hand side. The ask price is also called the offer price.

The bid price is the price that the buyer is willing to pay to buy the base currency, and represents the price at which you can sell.

The ask or offer price is the price that the seller is willing to sell the base currency, and represents the price at which you can buy.

The difference between the bid and the ask prices is referred to as the spread.

Figure 7.3 shows the bid and offer prices for the March 2011 Australian dollar futures contracts. The bid price is clearly 0.9737 and the ask price is 0.9739, a spread of 2 ticks.

Figure 7.3: Australian dollar futures March 2011 contract bid/ask values

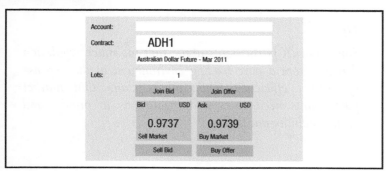

The bid/ask prices and spread are more transparent in the futures market than in the spot forex market because the same prices are essentially available to everyone as they are traded on a regulated exchange. Futures brokers act only to receive and execute orders for their clients. They do not act as principals or dealers in the way they do in the spot forex market, as discussed in chapter 5. Futures brokers do not add a margin or mark-up to the quoted prices and do not widen or alter spreads—they simply execute orders on behalf of the client and charge a commission for the provision of this service. They do not trade in the market as principals but as agents for their clients. Futures trades can be executed through a broker to whom you give verbal instruction to transact on your behalf, or on an electronic trading platform, where you place trades yourself.

Futures brokers are governed by the rules of the regulated exchanges on which futures contracts trade, and regulations are enforced by various governing bodies such as the National Futures Association (NFA) and the Commodity Futures Trading Commission (CFTC), both US organisations. The Chicago Mercantile Exchange (CME) group also has an in-house self-regulating market regulation department that aims to maintain a transparent and fair market place. Currency futures markets have a great deal more regulation, protection and oversight than the OTC spot forex market.

Tip

Some market participants argue that too much regulation detracts from a pure trading environment at the expense of market efficiency, while others claim that market participants need rules and regulations to protect and ensure stability and safety.

Margin and leverage

In order to trade currency futures you need a margin account with a licensed futures broker, who will direct orders to the exchange and transact on your behalf. Currency futures are traded on margin in order to maximise leverage, as we discussed in detail for the spot forex market in chapter 5. Without the use of margin, enormous amounts of cash would be required to participate in the currency futures market. The face value of the Australian dollar contract, as we have seen, is AUD100 000. By using a margin account, where a relatively small deposit is lodged and the balance borrowed from the broker, the buying power of our accounts increases markedly.

Tip

The amount of margin required for each futures contract is a function of volatility and is determined and set by the exchange clearing house.

The standard A$100 000 futures contract has, in late 2010, an initial margin requirement of US$3240. This means that in order to trade one standard contract the broker will require an initial margin of US$3240 to be lodged, or just over 3 per cent of the full value of the contract. The e-micro futures contract requires an initial margin of US$324, being one-tenth that of the full contract.

The margin lodged by the client with their broker is then lodged by the broker with the clearing house to insure the clearing house against any loss on the open position. This initial margin is also referred to as a security deposit or performance bond. It is essentially a good faith deposit that indicates you are willing and able to meet your obligations under the terms of the contract. Brokers are permitted to request higher margins from their clients than the minimums imposed by the exchange during volatile periods or if a client is perceived as a credit risk. Brokers are not allowed to apply a margin that is less than the minimum set by the exchange.

Tip

Trading on margin allows us to leverage our accounts to produce higher rates of return than would be possible without the use of leverage. Leverage also magnifies losses.

Let's look at an example of how trading on margin affects profits and losses.

With sufficient capital in our trading account to open a trade using a standard, or full-sized, Australian dollar currency futures contract, an initial margin deposit of US$3240 would be required. From our earlier example, the trade is entered long at 0.9867, and increases in value by 1 cent or 100 ticks to 0.9967. At US$10 per tick, the profit on the trade is US$1000. This represents a return of almost 31 per cent on the initial margin required for the trade, as we have made US$1000 profit by using just US$3240 of our own capital. Without the use of leverage the return would be 1 per cent — US$1000 profit on an investment of US$100 000.

The downside of leverage, of course, is that it can serve to greatly magnify losses, particularly for the unwary or over-eager trader who misuses leverage by taking on position sizes that are too large for their accounts. This will be discussed in chapter 9.

If the same trade had fallen by 100 ticks to 0.9767 from our initial long entry price of 0.9867, we have incurred a loss of $1000 on the trade, or minus 31 per cent return on the capital lodged as initial margin for the trade.

In addition to the initial margin required at the outset of a trade, a second margin called variation or maintenance margin is also required. Maintenance margin is part of the initial margin that must be maintained in cash in the trader's account while a trade remains open. It is generally a smaller amount than the initial margin.

Tip

If the cash balance in the trader's account at their futures broker falls below the maintenance level, a margin call will be issued, requiring the client to either add more cash to their account or liquidate the open position.

The novation process and the use of initial and maintenance margin go hand in hand. Currency futures contracts are essentially paper transactions that do not involve the sale or purchase of anything tangible. They are contracts for delivery of the specified commodity or currency at a date in the future, and physical delivery cannot take place before the specified date. Therefore, no money actually changes hands between the buyer and the seller no matter how many times contracts are bought and sold before the delivery date. The novation process of the clearing house acting as counterparty allows contracts to be bought and sold. The margin requirement in turn facilitates the novation process, allowing traders to buy and sell contracts by lodging margin with their futures broker.

As the price of the contract rises and falls, all open positions are re-valued at the end of each trading day in a process known as mark-to-market. If you have an open position that is in profit, the clearing house will credit your account. If you have an open position that is in loss, your trading account will be debited to maintain the margin requirement. If this loss amount totals more than the balance in cash in your account, a margin call will be issued. The whole process is seamless and ensures the transparent and efficient operation of futures trading.

Spot forex and currency futures compared

In chapters 5 and 6, we examined the spot forex market in detail, and in this chapter we have looked at currency futures. Both spot forex and currency futures provide retail traders with a means to access and trade the rapidly expanding forex market 24 hours a day, five and a half days per week. Both have advantages and disadvantages and we will now compare the two instruments to help you decide which is the more suitable market for you to trade in.

OTC versus regulated exchange

Spot forex trades in a non-regulated over-the-counter (OTC) market, while currency futures are traded on a regulated exchange. Spot forex has less regulation and there is no central market place where buyers and sellers are matched. The main downside to the OTC market is the potential risk of counterparty default. Currency futures trade on a regulated and centralised exchange where the exchange clearing house novates all trades by acting as buyer to every seller and seller to every buyer, which removes the risk of the counterparty defaulting.

Lot sizes and specifications

Spot forex can be traded in micro lots of 1000, mini lots of 10 000, and standard lots of 100 000 of the base currency, and multiples of these lot sizes. This provides access to the market to a huge array of traders, with large and small account balances, and provides for a much greater degree of flexibility than currency futures. The spot forex market allows those with relatively small account sizes to gain access to trading forex. Currency futures are traded in standard contract sizes of 100 000 and e-micro contracts of 10 000 of the base currency.

Currency futures have a fixed delivery or maturity date, when the currency specified in the contract must be physically delivered. Futures cannot be physically delivered before this date. In the spot forex market the initial delivery period is two days after the trade date, but the ability to roll over an open position at the close of each trading day effectively makes for a continuous contract.

Pips and ticks

Pip values in the spot forex market vary with the lot size being traded, providing traders with a huge amount of flexibility in regard to market and risk exposure in terms of each trade and each account. A trader with a very small account can trade one micro lot with a pip value of just 10 cents. As the account balance and the trader's experience grow, this can be increased to trading perhaps five micro lots or 50 cents per pip. Once the account balance has increased further, the trader may then choose to trade one mini lot at $1 per pip. Traders with larger accounts who are in a position to trade standard lots will do so at $10 per pip. But they may also choose to trade smaller amounts to reduce risk and exposure or to allow them to trade multiple positions. Either way, spot forex is extremely flexible when it comes to allocating trading capital and defining risk-management procedures.

Currency futures are somewhat less flexible in that they can only be traded in multiples of the available contract sizes, and the tick values are determined by these contract sizes. The smallest contract available is the e-micro contract, which has a minimum tick move of US$1, so traders with very small accounts may be prevented from using even the e-micro futures contracts.

Tip

Traders who have larger accounts—and are therefore in a position to trade standard futures contracts—may choose to use multiples of the smaller e-micros to provide flexibility in the management of their risk and their capital.

Brokers, dealers and market makers

Currency futures are traded through registered and licensed futures brokers who act as an agent for their clients. They accept orders to buy and sell from clients, and execute these orders on the appropriate exchange. This may be done manually, by placing the order verbally with the broker, or through the use of online electronic trading platforms to place orders. Brokers charge a commission for the provision of this service, and that is how they make their money. These commissions will vary between brokers and are generally negotiable depending on your level of trading activity and account balance.

In spot forex these services are provided by a market maker or a non-dealing desk firm, who both act as principal on behalf of the client into the larger inter-bank market. Both provide online trading platforms through which clients place buy and sell orders, or clients can place orders verbally. Market makers generally do not charge a commission, but may act as counterparty to their clients' trades, and may widen spreads and requote prices, as a way to make their money. Non-dealing desk, or direct market access, dealers may charge commission, but they generally add a mark-up to the best bid/offer prices they receive from their liquidity providers as their main means of generating revenue.

As a result, the price spread between the bid and the ask is *generally* narrower or tighter than in the spot forex market. We have discussed how the dealers and market makers in the spot forex market can use the bid/ask spread, and the various bid/ask quotes being supplied to them from the large banks, to widen and manipulate the spread and how, this can vary between dealing firms. In the currency futures market, what you see is what you get, as all brokers and traders see exactly the same price quotes on the regulated exchange.

Liquidity and transparency

Without doubt the volume traded on the spot forex market far outweighs the volume of currencies traded using currency futures. This makes spot forex a market place where it is extremely easy to enter and exit trades because of the huge volumes constantly being transacted. Average daily volumes in the currency futures are also great when compared with other financial markets and some commodities, but they are dwarfed by the volumes in the spot forex market, which turns over around US$4 trillion per day in 2010.

Transparency of price and volume is a major feature of currency futures that is not as available in the spot forex market, and is a major advantage for futures traders. Being able to see the depth of volume on the bid and ask, the order flow, and any outstanding orders provides a clear view as to the liquidity of the contract and the level of trader interest. Being able to see daily trading volumes in each currency futures contract on the exchange provides valuable information to traders about the liquidity of each contract and the market as a whole. Traders are able to see the actual bid and ask prices and the volumes being sought at each price level, no matter which broker or trading platform they are using—this information is available to all traders at all levels.

In contrast, bid and ask volumes and daily traded volumes are unavailable in the spot forex market because there is no central exchange on which this information can be reported and recorded. The decentralised nature of the spot forex market means that this information is not available for the market as a whole. Any of this information available from one dealing firm would be nowhere near comprehensive enough to reflect what could be happening in the rest of the market. Due to the nature of the spot forex market and the relationships that exist between various dealing firms and banks within the inter-bank market, price quotes can also show a degree of variation among different retail dealing firms and their platforms. Market-maker pricing may also vary considerably from the *real* price of the underlying instrument depending on spread calculations and price requotes.

Tip

In the currency futures market a small retail trader sees exactly the same price and volume information as a huge hedge fund.

Leverage and margin

Both spot forex and currency futures are traded using margin accounts and leverage, giving both groups access to large positions with the use of only a small amount of capital. The amount of leverage available in the spot forex market is far greater than in currency futures. It is possible to trade with up to 400:1 leverage in spot forex. These liberal and freely available leverage rates can provide the opportunity for spectacular gains—but also catastrophic losses. Currency futures are traded using much lower levels of leverage, generally in the vicinity of around 33:1. Trading futures generally requires the lodging of a larger initial margin deposit than spot forex. To open a standard Australian dollar currency futures contract currently requires a margin requirement of US$3240, while a standard AUD/USD lot size in the spot forex market could theoretically be opened with a margin of just US$250, using leverage of 400:1.

Tip

The lower level of immediately available leverage helps futures traders with their risk and money management.

It's all about choice

In choosing to trade forex, the two main instruments available to retail traders are spot forex and currency futures — both offer the ability to participate in the market as a speculator or hedger. Both are unique vehicles offering similar yet distinctly different products for participating in the forex market. Individual traders will have differing reasons for choosing one over the other, or they may decide to use both in different circumstances and with different strategies or trading methodologies. Either way, it is important that you know and understand the working of the two markets to allow you to make an informed decision.

Chapter summary

⇨ Currency futures have been available since their introduction by the Chicago Mercantile Exchange (CME) in 1972.

⇨ Price quotes are often referred to as being either European- or American-style quotes, which are based on historical trading conventions that have become internationally accepted standards. These terms reflect the position of the US dollar in the currency pair.

⇨ Aside from their use by traders and speculators, cross rates are important to companies and other entities trading on global markets that don't need exchange rates involving the US dollar.

⇨ Emerging market currency futures have been developed by the CME to allow traders to gain access to exchange rate markets that they are otherwise unable to trade, such as the Chinese yuan, Korean won and Russian rouble.

⇨ By interposing itself between the two counterparties to every trade, the clearing house guarantees that each trade will be honoured and settled as set out in the futures contract. This novation process means that buyers and sellers do not deal directly with each other and expose themselves to credit and counterparty default risk.

⇨ Unlike the decentralised over-the-counter spot forex market, currency futures are traded on a regulated exchange, such as the CME, and others that provide rules and regulations for trading in these financial products. As a result, currency futures contracts, like all futures contracts, have standard specifications — contract size, expiry or delivery date, and minimum price increment and corresponding value.

⇨ All futures contracts have a defined expiry date when they must be either delivered or settled in cash, depending on the terms of the contract.

⇨ Currency futures have a standard contract size expressed in the base currency.

⇨ Futures contracts indicate the minimum price increment that can occur, which is the tick value, or the smallest value by which the value of the contracts can change.

⇨ E-micro contracts are roughly one-tenth the size of standard currency futures contracts.

⇨ The bid/ask prices and spread are more transparent in the futures market than in the spot forex market because the same prices are essentially available to everyone as the contracts are traded on a regulated exchange.

⇨ Tthe two main instruments available to retail forex traders are spot forex and currency futures.

chapter 8

Macro economics and how it affects forex

Trading forex, with its high levels of liquidity, and the constant ebb and flow of buyers and sellers, is well suited to the use of technical analysis in its various forms. Technical analysis and the many indicators, oscillators, levels, patterns and moving averages, combined with price action, provide a multitude of trading signals for the proficient and effective trader.

Perhaps more than in any other market, a huge range of fundamental economic parameters and events affect the forex market. All forex traders need to be aware of the data and economic indicators that impact on currency exchange rates. It is also handy to have a grasp of the underlying strengths and weaknesses of the major global economies, and to have a general understanding of where they are in terms of the broader economic cycle. For each of the most commonly traded currencies, its unique characteristics and specific economic data and events have the most significant impact on their value.

This chapter takes a broad look at some of the economic data, events and indicators that influence currency values, and what happens to currency values when these economic indicators change either unexpectedly or in line with trader expectations. Economic data is released at set times and dates in the industrialised countries and these dates are known well in advance in most cases, providing a degree of certainty to the release of this information.

Tip

There is often a great deal of anticipation and speculation by traders in the lead-up to the release of data on the specified dates.

Other fundamental events that can impact currency markets include financial crises, political events and geo-political upheavals that are random and can occur unannounced at any time. Traders have no way of knowing about or preparing for these unexpected events and can only react to them after they have occurred.

We have already looked at the close relationship between interest rates and currency values in detail in chapter 2, so this chapter will focus on the other important economic indicators and events that impact directly on exchange rates.

Economic theory

There are a few well-known theories about what determines exchange rates. Like all economic theories, they work wonderfully well in the perfect world of research and analysis, when the realities of trading, including expectation, anticipation, speculation and the various other actions and reactions of humans, are omitted from the theory.

Purchasing power parity theory

Purchasing power parity (PPP) theory is based on the notion that the price of a product in one country should be equal to the price of the same product in another country when converted to a common currency. It is also referred to as the law of one price—any product traded on world markets will sell for the same price in every country when expressed in the same currency. If, for example, a laptop computer sells for A\$1000 in Australia then it should sell for US\$900 in the United States if the AUD/USD exchange rate is 0.9000 (US\$900 ÷ 0.900 = A\$1000).

PPP is calculated using this formula:

$$S = \frac{P_1}{P_2}$$

Where

S is the exchange rate of currency 1 to currency 2

P1 is the cost of the product in currency 1

P2 is the cost of the same product in currency 2

Tip

PPP is often referred to, tongue in cheek, as the Big Mac index.

The term Big Mac index is based on the global availability of Big Mac hamburgers, and the fact that similar inputs of domestically produced ingredients are used to produce a Big Mac. Therefore, under the PPP theory the price of a Big Mac hamburger should have the same base currency price the world over.

If the prices of the same goods are out of alignment, then this theory maintains that the relative values of the currencies should return to equilibrium. A change in the rate of inflation should be offset by a change in the opposite direction of the exchange rate, for instance. If prices are rising because of inflationary pressures, then the exchange rate should depreciate. If prices are falling, then the exchange rate should appreciate.

The reality is, however, quite different, as the PPP model makes no allowance for transportation costs, trade barriers, taxes and variations in production costs in different sectors in different economies. It also makes no allowance for interest rate differentials between countries.

Balance of payments theory

The balance of payments (BOP) is a measure of the payments that flow in and out of a country. The current account measures trade in goods and services, such as raw material exports and manufactured goods imports. The difference between imports and exports is referred to as the trade balance or the balance of trade. The capital account measures flows of money for financial transactions and investment.

Balance of payments theory holds that exchange rates should always return to an equilibrium level that produces a stable balance of payments. For example, a trade deficit that occurs when a country imports more than it exports needs to be offset by positive capital inflows so the current account and capital account balance each other out. The reality is that these inflows and outflows are never in perfect equilibrium, and other factors — such as inflation, unemployment levels and interest rates — are also drivers of exchange rates.

Tip

If more money flows into an economy than out of it, the country has a positive balance of payments or a trade surplus and the local currency will appreciate in value. If more money flows out of an economy than into it, the country has a negative balance of payments or a trade deficit and the local currency will depreciate in value.

Real interest rate differential theory

The basis of real interest rate differential theory is that a nation's interest rate is the major determinant of exchange rate movements. Currencies should appreciate in value in countries where interest rates are relatively high or rising, while currencies should depreciate in value in countries where interest rates are low or falling.

As interest rates rise, and the yield on the currency and other financial instruments in that country becomes more attractive to traders and investors, they will buy the currency. The currency will be in greater demand and the flow of capital into the country will increase. One of the key points stressed in the real interest rate differential model is the expectation of further interest rate increases, and the effect this will have on the strengthening of the currency. A shift in interest rate policy by the country's central bank that is expected to continue for a few years will have a much greater impact on the currency than a policy shift that is expected to be in place for only the short term.

This model puts great emphasis on capital flows and ignores the effects of geo-political and other crisis events that can upset the way traders and investors react towards high interest rates as the only determinant of a currency's value. While it is quite logical in theory for investors to gravitate towards investments that offer the highest rate of return, there is also a higher degree of risk or perceived risk. In times of global upheaval and uncertainty, investors will more often than not shift funds away from higher return/higher risk currencies and into lower risk, lower reward, safe-haven currencies, such as the US dollar, Japanese yen and Swiss franc, preferring the safety of their funds over the potential for higher returns.

Economic data and indicators that affect foreign exchange values

Let's now take a look at some of the major economic and other indicators, and the impact these have on foreign exchange markets and currency values. These indicators can be divided into economic indicators, inflation indicators and employment indicators. Whole books have been written on this subject, so this section provides just an overview.

Economic indicators provide a general overview of conditions within an economy, and paint the broad economic picture. They tend to be released at regular intervals, at known times and dates, allowing market players to watch and monitor the impact any changes in the values of these indicators will have on currency values.

Inflation indicators measure rising prices with an economy. Most central banks will use monetary policy measures, such as raising interest rates, to control inflation. Higher interest rates will generally lead to a rise in the value of the currency, so inflation is one of the most closely watched indicators. The inflation rate is also used to deflate nominal (or current) interest rates to real values (current rates adjusted for the effects of inflation).

Employment indicators are a measure of the structural soundness and underlying health of an economy. Low unemployment levels indicate a sound economy; high unemployment levels indicate a struggling or slow-paced economy.

Tip

Employment indicators are lagging indicators and are often the last to show changes in an economy.

As a country comes out of a recession or period of slower economic growth, new jobs are slowly added and this often takes a while to reflect in employment figures. If a country drops quickly into recession, jobs may be cut slowly, again taking some time to be reflected in the official unemployment numbers.

Countless economic releases bombard forex traders, and it is easy to get caught up in this endless stream of data and economic announcements. Economic releases can provide information on an event that has already happened based on past data (called a lagging indicator); an anticipated event in the future based on past data (called a leading indicator); or an event that is currently occurring based on current data and information (called a coincident indicator).

As the US dollar is still the most actively traded currency in the world, most traders have a keen interest in these indicators in the United States and the impact they have on the value of the US dollar. We will look at the major economic, inflation and employment indicators in detail for the US dollar, and then take a quick look at some of the fundamental indicators that affect other major currencies.

Economic indicators

Nine of the most widely watched and monitored economic indicators that have ramifications for forex traders are discussed here: gross domestic product (GDP), balance of trade, industrial production, durable goods orders, construction indicators, retail sales, the consumer confidence index, the

Institute for Supply Management index and the Conference Board Leading Economic Index®.

Gross domestic product

Gross domestic product (GDP) is considered to be one of the most important indicators of the health of an economy. It is a measure of all the goods and services produced in an economy within a 12-month period. GDP is a good measure of the overall size of an economy and is an effective way of comparing different economies around the world. The GDP for the United States is estimated by the International Monetary Fund (IMF) to be just over US$14 trillion in 2009. The next largest single-country economy is Japan, which has a GDP of just over US$5 trillion. In comparison the GDP figure for Australia estimated by the IMF is just under US$1 trillion, and for the Eurozone members, over US$16 trillion.

Tip

GDP growth is desirable as it indicates that an economy is expanding — consumers and governments are buying the goods and services being produced by businesses — and it is used as a measure of a country's standard of living.

The US GDP numbers are released by the Bureau of Economic Analysis (BEA) in three reports. The 'Advance Estimates' report is released at the end of the first month after the quarter for which the figures are being reported. This is followed a month later by the 'Preliminary' report, which contains more accurate information. The final GDP number is then released at the end of the third month after the end of the quarter for which the information is being reported. Currency traders watch the release of the advance estimates closely, as these numbers will indicate any changes occurring to the growth and overall health of the US economy.

A generally accepted rule of thumb is that GDP growth within an economy is sustainable over the long term at around 3 per cent per year. Growth any higher than this over an extended period begins to add to inflationary pressures. While a high rate of growth indicates a growing economy and will normally lead to an increase in the value of the currency, inflationary expectations also have a big impact. If market participants are fearful of an increase in inflation or inflationary expectations, this may have a negative impact on the currency.

Tip

GDP numbers are reported in current dollar values and constant dollar values. Constant dollar value reporting allows for comparisons to be easily made between historical periods as it factors out the effects of inflation.

The GDP data provides a detailed look at the overall economic health of an economy as it aims to represent the value of everything within an economy. As a result it also contains other information that helps paint a picture of what is occurring within sections of the economy. These include changes in government spending, private investment and personal consumption expenditure, which all indicate any rises and falls in spending and investment patterns, and in what areas an economy is expanding or contracting.

Balance of trade

The balance of trade is often referred to as net exports or trade balance as it measures the difference between the value of exports of, and international trade in, all goods and services in a given period. A trade surplus occurs when an economy exports more than it imports, which is generally considered favourable for an economy; a trade deficit, or trade gap, occurs when a country imports more than it exports, which is generally considered unfavourable for an economy. As the largest economy in the world by GDP, the US is both a huge importing and exporting nation that has run a trade deficit for many years. While the amount of this trade deficit varies in line with the performance of the US economy and the global economy as a whole, a long-lasting trade deficit adds to foreign debt, on which interest must be paid. The longer and larger a trade deficit remains in place, the more detrimental the effect on the currency. Traders watch the balance of trade for significant immediate change to the balance of trade and to monitor long-term trends.

Industrial production

Industrial production is the total output of the manufacturing, mining and utilities sector of the US economy. Although this sector is only a small contributor to GDP, it is an important measure of the strength of the economy because it is highly sensitive to consumer demand and interest rates, which flow through to the value of the currency. Strong consumer demand leads to higher levels of production, and thus a strong economy and a strong currency. Weak or reduced levels of industrial production caused by a slowing in consumer demand can indicate a slowing economy, which will have a negative impact on the value of the currency. Industrial production is also used as a measure of inflation, as high levels of industrial production can indicate high levels of consumer spending, leading to the potential for inflation and the need for monetary policy intervention to slow the economy.

Durable goods orders

Durable goods are products with a life span of more than three years. Examples include motor vehicles, household appliances, furniture, computers and machinery. This data is important for foreign exchange markets because it gives a good indication of consumer confidence. Businesses and individual consumers are more likely to buy durable goods when their confidence about the economy is high. If confidence is weak, then purchases of these larger goods tend to be delayed. A high number for durable goods orders, therefore, indicates a propensity for retail and industrial consumers to spend their money, adding to economic growth and adding to the value of the currency. A low number indicates consumers are not confident and so not spending, which slows growth and weakens the currency.

Tip

Durable goods orders is one of the earliest indicators of the underlying conditions within an economy, as this figure reflects consumer's commitment to spending money on big ticket items, which in turn affects levels of manufacturing activity.

Construction indicators

Housing has traditionally been the driving force behind the US economy, and often leads the country out of recession. These indicators are classified into three major categories:

⇨ housing starts and permits—the total number of new housing projects begun each month

⇨ existing home sales—sales of previously owned single family homes

⇨ new home sales—sales of newly built homes that have not been previously occupied.

Construction indicators are cyclical and sensitive to the level of interest rates (mortgage rates) and the level of disposable income. Low interest rates and high levels of consumer confidence generally lead to increased new and existing home sales. Low interest rates alone, however, may not be enough to generate a high demand for new housing. Lack of job security and a weak or struggling economy will result in low rates of housing construction despite low interest rates. This reflects the situation in the US in 2009–10, where historically low interest rates have failed to stimulate housing construction, because of high unemployment levels, lack of job security and weak consumer confidence.

Tip

In the US housing starts between one and a half and two million units tend to indicate a strong economy, whereas a figure of less than one million units suggests that the US economy is in, or headed for, a recession. The US Census Bureau and the Department of Housing and Urban Development estimated that the seasonally adjusted annual rate of housing starts in October 2009 was 529 000.

Retail sales

Retail sales is an estimate of the sale of all durable and non-durable goods in the US. Personal consumption spending accounts for more than 65 per cent of the United States' GDP, so retail sales figures are watched closely by forex traders as an indicator of what and how much consumers are spending, and as a gauge of consumer confidence. If consumer confidence is high and the economic outlook healthy, these factors will be reflected in strong numbers for retail sales, which will have a positive impact on the currency. Weaker numbers, indicating a slowing economy or a more cautious outlook by consumers, or both, may impact negatively on the currency, as an economic slowdown may be imminent. If the retail sales number grows too quickly, then demand may outpace supply, causing prices to rise and adding to inflationary expectations and the possible use of a rise in interest rates to slow the economy. If, however, the economy has been in a period of slower growth and inflation is not a cause for concern, then an increase in retail sales will be seen as very bullish for the economy and the currency.

Consumer confidence index

The consumer confidence indicator (CCI) is a monthly nation-wide survey of 5000 different households each month in the US that aims to gauge the views of the average consumer on the current state of the economy, as well as expectations for the future. Three separate figures make up the CCI:

⇨ index of consumer sentiment — how respondents currently feel about their current financial position

⇨ current economic conditions — how they feel the general economy is going

⇨ index of consumer expectations — how they feel the economy will be in six months' time.

Tip

The consumer confidence index, or CCI, is a sentiment indicator that tends to be at the forefront of tracking the business cycle, as it represents what the average consumer is thinking and feeling about the economy.

It is, however, a highly subjective survey with a relatively small sample size that at times can be highly influenced by emotive issues, such as petrol prices and other matters that may be pertinent at the time the survey is completed. Market watchers and analysts tend to look at averages of the index over extended periods rather than the data for each month. If consumers are happy and feel their standard of living is improving, this will be reflected in the survey. If the CCI is rising in line with increasing retail sales and other consumer-driven indicators, then it is the sign of a strong economy.

Institute for Supply Management Index

The Institute for Supply Management (ISM) Index is a monthly index that measures the activity of 300 nationwide purchasing managers in the manufacturing and industrial sectors. They are surveyed on their current activities, including production levels and capacity, inventory levels, new orders, employment and other manufacturing-related activities. Survey participants are asked a series of questions to which they can only respond in one of three ways: better, the same or worse. These responses are then used to construct the survey results and to compare them with responses from the previous month. Index values above 50 indicate expansion within the sector and the overall economy over the previous month, while values under 50 indicate a contracting economy. Figures that come in above market estimates and expectations will result in a rally in the price of the US dollar; the release of figures lower than market expectations will result in a selloff in the US dollar.

Even though the US economy, like most of the major world economies, is now a service-based economy, the ISM Index is still extremely important. The manufacturing sector still plays a big role in the US economy, so the employment and prices-paid sections of the index provide valuable information on the labour market and inflation.

Tip

The ISM Index is considered a leading indicator because it provides a view of what the leading industrial and manufacturing companies are currently doing and anticipate doing in the months ahead.

Conference Board Leading Economic Index®

The Conference Board Leading Economic Index (LEI) is calculated by the Conference Board, a non-government organisation, and is a leading indicator that combines much of the information from the surveys and indexes conducted by various government and non-government organisations we have discussed previously. It is a composite index that combines information from 10 individual components, which is intended to provide an insight into where the US economy is headed several months in advance. It is seen as a smoothed index because it is a combination of the following 10 components, which removes the volatility of any one individual component:

⇨ average weekly hours worked in the manufacturing sector

⇨ average weekly initial claims for unemployment benefits

⇨ manufacturer's new orders for consumer goods and materials

⇨ index of supplier deliveries—a measure of the speed of delivery of new merchandise from suppliers to vendors

⇨ manufacturer's new orders for non-defence capital goods

⇨ building permits for new private housing

⇨ stock prices based on the S&P 500 Index

⇨ inflation-adjusted M2 money supply—a measure of the total amount of money in circulation in an economy

⇨ the spread or difference between long-term and short-term government bond interest rates

⇨ consumer sentiment index.

Generally speaking an increase in the value of the index is positive for the US economy and the US dollar, and a decrease in the value of the index is negative for the economy and the value of the US dollar.

Inflation indicators

The economic indicators discussed earlier provide us with information on growth and changes within an economy. The inflation indicators discussed following are used to gauge the level of price stability within an economy.

Consumer price index

A consumer price index (CPI) is a measure of the average price of consumer goods and services purchased by households within an economy. It measures the average change in prices paid for a constant basket of goods and services from one period to the next within the same area. It is compiled from a sample of prices for food, shelter, fuel, clothing, transportation and medical services.

The percentage change in the CPI is the main measure for estimating inflation, or price growth, within an economy and changes in the cost of living. Rapid increases in the value of the CPI indicate inflation; rapid decreases can suggest the onset of deflation—a decrease in the price of goods and services leading to low or no economic growth. Economists and other market analysts tend to focus on the CPI-U figure in the United States. The CPI-U figure, or the core inflation rate, excludes food and energy components from the measurement, as these tend to be the most volatile and seasonal prices.

The US Federal Reserve, like all central banks, closely monitors the CPI as its main indicator of inflation within the economy. Sudden or unpredicted changes to the CPI lead to sharp increases in currency market volatility as traders react to changes in the CPI number in anticipation of moves by the central bank to keep inflation under control.

Producer price index

The producer price index (PPI) is a collection of indices that measure price changes by domestic producers, and how the producers' cost of materials can be passed on to consumers in the form of higher prices for their finished goods. The PPI measures price changes from the business side as opposed to the CPI, which measures price changes from the consumer side — what businesses are charging rather than what people are paying for products.

The PPI records changes in prices in percentage terms over the previous recording period for a wide range of industries in the US economy, including manufacturing, mining, agriculture, forestry, fishing and energy production. It is a broad-based indicator that reflects changes in production costs across virtually the whole US economy, providing a valuable insight into any inflationary pressures that may be starting to build. If producers are paying more for their inputs, these costs will be passed on to consumers, which in turn affects the CPI.

Commodity Research Bureau Futures Index

The Commodity Research Bureau Futures Index (CRB Index) measures changes in the prices of 17 commodities actively traded on US futures exchanges; these commodities are raw materials or products that are associated with the beginning stages of production. Prices of these materials are among the first to react to changing economic conditions. The CRB Index is an early indicator of changes in the business climate and inflation. The index is also an actively traded futures contract, so tracking changes in the value of the index is simply a matter of monitoring changes in the price of the CRB futures contract. The commodities included in the CRB Index and their sub-group weightings within the index are shown in table 8.1 (overleaf).

Table 8.1: components of the CRB Index and their weighting in the index

Sub-group	Sub-group weight	Commodities
Energy	17.60%	Crude oil
		Heating oil
		Natural gas
Grains	17.60%	Wheat
		Corn
		Soybeans
Industrials	11.80%	Copper
		Cotton
Meats	11.80%	Live cattle
		Lean hogs
Softs	23.50%	Coffee
		Cocoa
		Sugar
		Orange juice
Precious metals	17.60%	Gold
		Silver
		Platinum

The CRB Index makes it relatively easy to watch for changes in commodity prices and inflationary trends.

Employment indicators

The unemployment rate is a lagging economic indicator, as it tends to change more slowly than many other economic indicators, particularly during times of recession. Once an economic contraction has caused jobs to be cut, it often takes time for consumer confidence to return before old jobs are filled again or new jobs created. Employment reports are of major importance to all financial markets, and to the forex market in particular, as they paint a very clear picture of the underlying health of any economy. Decreasing unemployment signals a strong economy with a positive impact on the currency. Increasing unemployment signals a weaker economy with a negative impact on the currency. There are two main measures of employment in the US: non-farm payrolls and the employment cost index.

Non-farm payrolls

Non-farm payrolls (NFP) identifies the total number of paid workers, excluding those working in agriculture, in the US and measures the number of jobs added or lost in the economy over the preceding month. NFP numbers are released monthly by the US Department of Labor, providing an ongoing statement on the underlying health of the US economy. The farming sector is excluded from the data because of the seasonal nature of the industry, which would distort the numbers around seasonal harvest times when workers are added and then laid off at the completion of harvest.

In general, an increase in employment (decrease in unemployment), measured by an increase in the number of paid workers, indicates businesses are hiring more workers because they are expanding. More people employed means more money to spend on goods and services produced by these businesses, fuelling economic growth, and so the spiral continues. A decrease in employment (increase in unemployment) indicates jobs are being lost as the economy contracts. Fewer people employed means less money to spend, fuelling further job cuts, and so the downward spiral continues.

Non-farm payrolls is the most closely watched of all the economic indicators we have discussed because of the impact job creation or job losses have on the economy as a whole. Much of this importance can be considered political as well as purely economic because of the pressure on the Federal

Reserve and the US government to maintain employment levels. Interest rate policies are also heavily influenced by the rate of employment, with the Fed less likely to raise interest rates when unemployment levels are high or rising.

As well as the overall number of jobs added or lost the NFP report also includes data on:

⇨ the unemployment rate as a percentage of the overall workforce

⇨ the sectors that are showing increases or decreases in levels of employment

⇨ average hourly earnings.

Average hourly earnings is important because if the same number of people remain employed, but are earning less money through working fewer hours, then this is effectively an increase in unemployment.

Tip

Revisions of the NFP numbers can also move the currency markets in response to revised levels of employment or unemployment.

Employment Cost Index

The Employment Cost Index (ECI) is a quarterly report that details changes in the cost of labour in the US. It is both an inflation and an employment indicator as it measures whether the cost of employment is rising or falling, thus measuring wage inflation. The US Federal Reserve uses shifts in the ECI in its decisions to adjust interest rates. The ECI is a widely monitored and reported economic indicator that seldom makes headlines, despite its importance to traders and market analysts.

Important economic indicators for the major global economies

In keeping with our discussion of the seven most highly traded and important global currencies, we will now take a brief look at some of the important economic indicators that affect the other six currencies. As interest rate, employment, inflation and GDP announcements for each economy tend to have similar, if not the same, ramifications for each currency we will only look at economic indicators that are unique to each country.

Important economic indicators for the Eurozone

According to the IMF, if the Eurozone was a single country it would have the largest economy by GDP in the world, surpassing the GDP of the United States by more than US$2 trillion—the combined GDP of the member countries of the Eurozone is in excess of US$16 trillion. The euro is also the second most actively traded currency, and for that reason a number of economic indicators related to the Eurozone are closely watched by forex traders. The Eurozone also contains four of the top 10 countries by GDP in the world. It is important to monitor these indicators for specific member countries, particularly the large GDP countries of Germany and France, as well as monitoring them for the Eurozone as a whole.

The nature of the Eurozone means that there is a range of economic climates, from some of the world's largest to some very small economies, which are combined to produce the headline figures for the Eurozone as a whole. For this reason, emphasis tends to be placed on the data and figures for Germany, France and Italy, as the combined GDP of these three countries makes up more than half the GDP for the Eurozone as a whole. The GDP of the individual Eurozone member countries is shown in table 8.2 (overleaf).

Table 8.2: Eurozone countries and their gross domestic product (GDP), 2009

Country	GDP in millions of US$	World rank by GDP
Germany	3 338 675	4th
France	2 656 378	5th
Italy	2 118 264	7th
Spain	1 467 889	9th
Netherlands	796 651	16th
Belgium	472 103	20th
Austria	382 073	23rd
Greece	330 780	27th
Finland	238 607	34th
Portugal	233 478	35th
Ireland	222 156	38th
Slovakia	88 210	60th
Luxembourg	52 432	68th
Slovenia	48 600	70th
Cyprus	23 603	91st
Malta	8008	128th

Source: International Monetary Fund world economic outlook data 2009.

Some of the most important economic indicators for the Eurozone include the Harmonised Index of Consumer Prices (HCIP), German Ifo Survey, German ZEW Survey, National Institute of Statistics and Economic Studies (French INSEE), and PMI (Purchasing Manager Indexes).

Harmonised Index of Consumer Prices

Each member country must provide information on more than 100 indexes used to calculate the Harmonised Index of Consumer Prices (HICP) as a monthly measurement of prices and inflation across the Eurozone. These national figures are weighted before arriving at the final aggregate figure. The HICP is released after the CPI figures for the individual member countries.

Tip

The HCIP is important because it is the reference point used by the European Central Bank to monitor inflation.

German Ifo Survey

This survey is conducted monthly by the Ifo Institute for Economic Research at the University of Munich. Each month the survey queries 7000 German firms on the current business climate and their expectations for the next six months. As Germany is the largest economy in the Eurozone, this survey is a significant indicator for the overall economic health of the Eurozone. The index uses a base value of 100, which represents the average balance in the year 2000, when the survey began. The further the monthly value is away from 100 the stronger or weaker the sentiment, with positive readings indicating a strong economy and negative readings indicating a slowdown.

German ZEW Survey

ZEW is the acronym for the Centre for European Economic Research. It conducts a monthly survey of more than 350 financial analysts from firms in finance, trading and investment, predominantly in Germany. The Economic Sentiment Indicator is the headline component of the survey and is based on answers to the single question: 'In the medium term (six months) the overall macroeconomic situation will: improve / no change / worsen / no estimation?' The resulting figure is the difference between positive and negative responses. The ZEW is considered as one of the most important economic data releases for the Eurozone and the results of the survey have a significant impact on the euro.

National Institute of Statistics and Economic Studies (French INSEE)

The institute's French Business Survey covers 4000 French firms across a broad spectrum of industries, from agriculture to manufacturing. Firms are surveyed on current and forecast output, inventory levels, actual prices received or paid over the preceding three months, and estimated prices for the next three months. The figures are used to measure inflation and other variables within the French economy. While it is not as important as the German Ifo or the ZEW surveys, the figures help to paint a broad picture of the Eurozone economy as a whole.

PMI (Purchasing Manager Indexes)

Similar to the ISM index in the US, these indexes provide a view of business conditions across the Eurozone. The PMI show the results of a monthly survey by the Institute of Supply Management of 5000 firms across the Eurozone on five main factors—new orders, production levels, employment conditions, inventory levels and supplier deliveries. Indices are calculated for sectors (manufacturing, retail, services), individual countries and the Eurozone. The Eurozone PMI is a composite number that provides a sense of the broader outlook across the Eurozone for a wide spectrum of businesses and economic conditions. A value above 50 indicates expansion, and a value below 50 indicates contraction in the sectors, individual countries, or Eurozone as a whole.

Other economic indicators

Other economic indicators that are relevant to changes in currency values, but don't impact as dramatically on forex markets, include:

⇨ German Consumer Confidence

⇨ Eurozone Economic Sentiment Indicator (ESI)

⇨ Eurozone retail trade figures

⇨ Eurozone trade balance

⇨ German and Eurozone industrial production.

Important economic indicators for Japan

Japan is the second-largest country by GDP and a large exporting nation, and it has the third most actively traded global currency. Some of the unique indicators for the Japanese economy that forex traders need to be aware of are the Tankan Survey, the trade balance and the Industrial Production index.

Tankan Survey

The Tankan Survey is conducted by the Bank of Japan, the country's central bank, four times each year on around 9000 Japanese firms. It provides valuable insights into the overall economic outlook for the Japanese economy, including the business sector outlook on capital expenditure, prices and employment.

Tip

The Tankan Survey is used by the Bank of Japan in formulating its monetary policy and is widely watched and anticipated by forex traders.

Trade balance

As Japan's economy is highly export driven, the balance of payments and the trade balance numbers can provide a valuable insight into any changes occurring within the Japanese economy. A surplus trade balance indicates capital is flowing into Japan as foreign consumers purchase Japanese exports; this has a positive impact on the yen. A trade deficit indicates exports have slowed and that Japan is importing more than it is exporting, which will have a negative impact on the value of the yen. The monthly merchandise trade balance that excludes services is a more accurate measure of Japan's visible trade in cars and electronics in exchange for raw material to manufacture these goods.

Industrial Production Index

The Industrial Production (IP) Index measures changes in the output of Japanese domestic mining, manufacturing and utility companies and does not include any data on imports. It is an index of domestic production for sales either within Japan or for export and provides a view on Japanese domestic economic conditions.

Other indicators for Japan

Other relevant economic indicators for forex traders include:

⇨ Japanese tertiary industry index

⇨ leading economic index

⇨ monthly retail trade index

⇨ Bank of Japan monthly report

⇨ household spending.

Important economic indicators for the United Kingdom

The British pound is the fourth most actively traded currency, and it has a checkered relationship with the euro and the Eurozone. Some of the important indicators for the UK and the British pound are the trade balance, industrial production and new housing starts.

Trade balance

As one of the largest components of the UK's balance of payments, the trade balance provides a view of the difference between British exports and imports and any impending changes to the pound as a result of a trade surplus or deficit. The non–European Union trade balance provides details of Britain's trade with countries outside Europe and how currency pairs trading against the pound may be affected by changes in the trade surplus or deficit.

Industrial Production Index

The Industrial Production (IP) Index measures changes in domestic output from mining, manufacturing and energy companies for domestic and export use, which represents around a quarter of Britain's GDP. It is a well-recognised indicator for measuring the level of domestic industrial activity. High or rising figures indicate increased production, leading to economic expansion, which benefits the pound. Over-production may also indicate the potential for inflation, which will have negative effects on the pound.

New housing starts

Like many Western economies the housing market is a key driver of the economy in the UK, so changes to the numbers of new houses being built provide an insight into the underlying health of the economy.

Other indicators for the United Kingdom

Other indicators to watch for the UK include:

⇨ retail sales

⇨ nationwide consumer confidence.

Important economic indicators for Australia

As a major exporter of raw materials and importer of finished goods, the balance of trade figures are particularly important to the Australian economy and the value of the Australian dollar. Both retail sales figures and the trade balance are watched closely by forex traders.

Trade balance

As the measure of the difference between exports and imports, this figure has particular importance for the Aussie dollar. When exports are greater than imports and the Australian economy is in trade surplus, the Australian dollar increases in value. When imports are greater than exports and the economy is in a trade deficit, the Australian dollar decreases in value. As a result, the Australian dollar tends to have an inverse relationship with other major currencies, rising when they are falling as exports increase and often falling when the other majors are strong and exports fall off. The demand for Australia's raw materials to fuel global economic growth also sees the Aussie dollar rally when demand for commodities and other raw materials is high.

Tip

Forex traders watch the Australian trade balance and other trade-related figures closely to monitor any changes in exports and imports.

Retail trade

This is a measure of all sales of goods and services by retail outlets within Australia. It is an important measure of consumer spending patterns and impending inflationary pressures within the Australian economy. Steadily rising retail sales will also lead to greater imports to meet demand, with a negative impact on the balance of trade.

Other indicators for Australia

Other indicators to watch for the Australian economy are:

⇨ Westpac Consumer Confidence survey

⇨ new motor vehicle sales

⇨ Housing Industry of Australia new home sales.

Important economic indicators for Switzerland

With a small population and limited natural resources, foreign trade is important to the Swiss economy, so the trade balance is a closely monitored figure, as it is in all industrialised economies. The Swiss franc is also considered a safe-haven currency during turbulent economic times. The UBS Consumption Indicator (compiled by the Swiss investment bank UBS) and retail sales are watched by forex traders.

UBS Consumption Indicator

This monthly indicator is calculated by combining the results of new car sales, overnight hotel stays within Switzerland by Swiss nationals, credit card transactions, a consumer sentiment index and a retail trends index. The results are combined into an index that is used to gauge the strength of domestic demand and the health of the Swiss economy. A rising value indicates increasing consumer spending, leading to economic growth, while a decrease tends to signal a contraction in the economy. A rapid rise in the index also signals rising inflationary pressures. The value is always positive so the current value of the index is compared with the previous month's values, as well as the short-term and long-term average values to monitor changes.

Adjusted retail sales

Because private consumption is a large component of Swiss GDP, retail sales tend to be a leading indicator for the Swiss economy. Increasing consumer spending may indicate impending inflationary pressures, which will have a negative impact on the Swiss franc.

Important economic indicators for Canada

Canada is a commodity- and export-driven economy with the world's seventh most actively traded currency. Forex traders monitor a number of trade-related economic indicators for the Canadian dollar, particularly the International Merchandise Trade, Ivey Purchasing Managers Index and retail sales.

International Merchandise Trade

International Merchandise Trade (IMT) reports on the difference between imports and exports of tangible goods, such as oil, gold and manufactured goods, which are some of the major contributors to Canada's GDP. IMT figures differ from the trade balance because they don't include intangibles or services. A trade surplus indicates funds are flowing into the Canadian economy and contributing to the appreciation of the value of the Canadian dollar, while a trade deficit indicates funds are flowing out of the Canadian economy, which will generally depreciate the value of the Canadian dollar.

Ivey Purchasing Managers Index

Across Canada, 175 corporate executives respond monthly to the Ivey Purchasing Managers Index (PMI) survey question: 'Are you purchasing higher, the same, or lower than the previous month?' Responses are collated into an index where a number above 50 indicates an increase in purchases over the previous month (expansion of the economy), and a number below 50 indicates a decrease in purchases from the previous month (contraction of the economy).

The PMI is a measure of optimism within the business community and an indicator of economic growth. If firms are increasing purchases in response to increased demand for their goods and services, then the economy is expanding. If this is reflected in an optimistic outlook, then it is a good indicator of expected future economic conditions.

Retail sales

This report is a direct measure of consumer confidence and is a leading indicator for most Western economies. If consumers are spending more it indicates confidence and the prospect of increased future growth, with a positive impact on the economy and the currency. If consumer spending is contracting, it indicates lower levels of confidence and the prospect of slower economic growth, with negative repercussions for both the economy and the currency.

Other indicators for Canada

Other economic indicators to watch for Canada include:

⇨ building permits

⇨ housing starts

⇨ new motor vehicle sales.

Tip

More often than not, markets anticipate the figures that will be announced before the actual release of the numbers for any of these economic indicators. As a result, reactions and price movements are triggered if the announced figures are not in line with these expectations.

Chapter summary

⇨ A huge range of fundamental parameters and economic events affect the forex market. It is important for all forex traders to be aware of the data and economic indicators that influence currency exchange rates.

⇨ Purchasing power parity (PPP) is based on the theory that the price of a product in one country should be equal to the price of the same product in another country when converted to a common currency.

⇨ The balance of payments (BOP) is a measure of the payments that flow into and out of a country. The current account measures trade in goods and services, such as raw material exports and manufactured goods imports. The difference between imports and exports is referred to as the trade balance. The capital account measures flows of money for financial transactions and investment.

⇨ The basis of real interest rate differential theory is that a nation's interest rate is the major determinant of exchange rate movements.

⇨ Economic indicators provide a general overview of conditions within an economy, and paint a broad economic picture. They tend to be released at regular intervals at known times and dates, allowing market players to monitor the impact any changes in the values of these indicators will have on currency values.

⇨ Inflation indicators measure rising prices with an economy. Most central banks will use monetary policy measures, such as increasing interest rates, to control inflation. Higher interest rates will generally lead to a rise in the value of the currency, so inflation is one of the most closely watched indicators for forex traders. The inflation rate is also used to deflate nominal interest rates to real values.

⇨ Employment indicators are a measure of the structural soundness and underlying health of an economy. Low unemployment levels indicate a sound economy, while high unemployment levels indicate a struggling or slow-paced economy.

⇨ Gross domestic product (GDP) is considered to be one of the most important indicators of the health of an economy.

⇨ Durable goods orders is one of the earliest indicators of the underlying conditions within an economy, as it reflects consumer commitment to spend money on big ticket items, which in turn affects levels of manufacturing activity.

⇨ Housing has traditionally been the driving force behind the US economy and often leads it out of recession.

⇨ A consumer price index (CPI) is a measure for estimating the average price of consumer goods and services purchased by households within an economy. It measures the average change in prices paid for a constant basket of goods and services from one period to the next within the same area.

⇨ The unemployment rate is a lagging economic indicator, as it tends to change more slowly than many other economic indicators, particularly during times of recession.

chapter 9

Money management for forex

As for all trading endeavours in all markets, the most critical yet most often overlooked component is money management. All too often traders are focused on the next great entry technique, the whiz-bang new indicator or some other approach that is set to make them a successful and wealthy trader. And all too often this ends in tears, because they take risks that are too big for the money they have, have not planned for a losing streak, have not accepted the fact that they will have losing trades, and do not understand the full implications of trading on margin using leverage, as discussed in chapter 5. In this chapter we will delve into many of the concepts involved in risk management and money management in general, and more specifically how they can be applied to the spot forex market with its unique leverage opportunities.

Not all trades will be winners and many will be losers. If we don't accept this fact then we are doomed to fail in the markets. To be successful as a trader requires an acceptance of being a loser, sometimes on several occasions in a row, when trades go against us.

Tip

The broad subject of money management can be broken down into three main areas — capital preservation and growth; the setting of stop losses, and the use of trailing stops or profit targets or both; and position-sizing techniques to ensure appropriate use and management of leverage and margin.

Swinging for the fences

The first step towards becoming a successful and profitable trader, and building a solid foundation from which to approach the markets with a sound money management plan, is setting realistic expectations in terms of time, profit and return on capital. All too often people entering the markets, and in particular the spot forex market, expect to become profitable and successful traders within about three weeks, with a starting account balance of less than $10 000. A huge number of people — on the internet and in other media sources, and through some trading education companies, and providers of unverified signal services — claim they have turned small amounts of capital into hundreds of thousands, even millions, of dollars. While some of these claims may well be realistic, many are not. Unfortunately people are tempted into the markets by these claims, or set out to emulate these claims, only to find that in the vast majority of cases the claims being made are simply unrealistic. In some cases the figures and results have been fabricated and are unsubstantiated, and the claimed results cannot be verified. In other cases the results may have been achieved, but the starting capital required to achieve the claimed results is beyond the realms of the average retail trader.

Plenty of traders do consistently achieve returns that are well above the average levels of returns that investors have come to expect from the equity markets and other, more passive, investment fields. However, these people have been trading for considerable amounts of time and have developed an enormous amount of experience and skill through long involvement in the markets. Most consistently successful traders are not over-night sensations; instead they are long-term survivors who use a disciplined approach and a strict set of rules for their trading, which they adhere to without fail. They employ strict money management rules that allow them to maximise returns for their time, effort and capital. They are not looking for one winning trade where they have thrown all their trading capital and miraculously achieved a winning trade that will allow them to retire to a secluded island paradise by 5 pm next Friday. They understand that trading is a game of probabilities in which there will be winning and losing trades, winning streaks and losing streaks, and periods of euphoria as well as periods of gloom. They have a tempered approach to all of the variables the market can throw at them because they know that if they persevere and keep following their trading and money management rules they will achieve success and above-average returns over the long run.

Tip

Successful traders are realistic in their expectations.

Too often, beginner traders are sold the story that with a starting balance of less than $10 000 they will be able to replace their existing weekly income or be able to fully support themselves from their trading activities within a short period of time. That's not likely to happen.

Let's look at an example and assume that the average single person needs about $40 000 per year to live a comfortable lifestyle with all bills able to be paid without any stress and have some holidays through the year as well. If this person launches into a trading career, having quit their job, with a $10 000 starting balance, they need to return 400 per cent per year just to maintain their lifestyle, and they haven't paid any tax yet! If they also wanted to increase the amount of working capital they have available and grow their account balance, they have to achieve well in excess of 400 per cent per annum year after year after year. Compare this with a trader who begins trading with a $100 000 account balance: this trader has to achieve 40 per cent return per year to maintain their $40 000 per year lifestyle income, or someone who starts out with $200 000 and requires a 20 per cent return to achieve the required $40 000 yearly income

The main problem is that the trader who starts out with a small amount of capital will start 'swinging for the fences' — taking excessive risk, using large position sizes as they try to achieve their goal, hoping for one or two trades that will get them over the line. But instead of making winning trades, they are much more likely to see their accounts fairly quickly decay to a point where it is no longer viable to trade. Table 9.1 shows the percentage return required to get your starting capital back to its original level after a percentage capital loss. It highlights the often overlooked fact of how hard it actually is to make back your capital, particularly if you suffer a significant loss of that capital.

Tip

An initial goal for all traders when starting out must simply be the preservation of capital while they learn the new skills needed to become a successful trader.

Table 9.1: percentage gain needed to recover capital loss in trading

Percentage loss of capital	Percentage return needed to recover
5	5.3
10	11.1
20	25
25	33
50	100
60	150
75	300

If you start out with $10 000 and lose $6000 through poor or no money management, you have lost 60 per cent of your account. In order for you to return your account to the $10 000 you started out with you need to make a 150 per cent return on the $4000 left in your account. Put another way, you will have to be two and a half times more successful in your attempts to make back your losses than you were when you made the losses initially — a big call!

Many traders do not understand this concept of the importance of capital preservation. If you lose your capital you can't trade any more. This lack of knowledge and understanding causes them to go after 'the home run trade' as they seek to rapidly expand their trading capital or strive too hard to achieve an above average return on their capital. This lack of understanding causes many traders to take risks that are too large for the size of their account and is one of the major contributing factors in the failure of many new traders. Much of this can be attributed to a lack of understanding of the use of stop losses and trailing stops to clearly define the amount of money that can be lost on *every* trade, before the trade is undertaken, and a lack of understanding of appropriate position-sizing techniques to ensure that the amount of capital being put at risk on every trade is relative to the account size and the individual trader's risk profile.

Defining losses

Traders must clearly define the amount of capital they are prepared to lose on each trade. While traders spend a huge amount of time and effort defining their trade entry rules and requirements, they often overlook the concept of trade exit or at best give it only minor consideration. Defining the point at which a trade will be exited separates the real traders from the punters.

Tip

Knowing how to accept losing trades, through the application of clearly defined exit rules, will go a long way towards contributing to your long-term trading success.

Often referred to as cutting your losses, having clearly defined exit rules is simply knowing when you will admit that a trade is not working out as planned, accept that the market has moved against you, and cut or exit the trade. It is all about accepting defeat, accepting that on this occasion you are wrong, and moving on to the next trade. There is no point hanging on to losing positions in the hope that they will turn around and move back in your favour. This not only ties up your capital in a losing trade that you can't put to better use in another potentially profitable trading opportunity, but also wastes mental energy as you struggle with what to do with the trade, and spend precious time agonising over when to do it. Far better to cut the losing trade early and unemotionally, and move on to the next potentially profitable opportunity—setting up a stop loss will allow you to do this.

Tip

The point at which a trade will be exited for an initial loss is referred to as a stop loss. It is the point at which the amount of money we can afford to lose on any trade is reached and the trade is cut or exited in order to stop any further loss of capital.

Setting stop-loss levels

In order to work effectively, stop-loss levels must be clearly defined for each trade *before* the trade is placed in the market. Every trade must be entered knowing exactly where it will be exited if the trade goes the wrong way. This process ensures we know how much money we are prepared to lose on a trade and the price at which this event will occur. Once that price point is reached the trade is exited immediately, either manually if you are executing the trades yourself, or automatically if you are using is a fully automated mechanical trading system, without a second thought or any emotional engagement.

If you are wrong, move on—there is no point trying to hang on to a losing trade to prove a point or to prove to the market or anyone else that you know what you are doing. No-one gets every trade right every time. Even the greatest traders in the world have losing trades. What makes them great traders, however, is that they know they will have losing trades, accept their losses, and know precisely where these trades will be exited. This process allows them to continually probe the market in search of profitable trading opportunities. By cutting losing trades early, they are able to allocate the capital to another potentially profitable trading opportunity, as well as ridding themselves of any attachment to the outcome of any one trade.

Tip

The number-one trading rule is to always trade with an initial stop loss and place it when you open every new trade.

The level of stop losses can be determined in a number of ways, and you may want to research the most appropriate method for you. Some methods include:

⇨ using a maximum dollar amount expressed as a percentage of your trading account. If you have a $10 000 account, for example, you may wish to set, say, 3 per cent, or $300, as the maximum loss you are prepared to accept on any losing trade. Generally, the larger your account size, the smaller this amount is in percentage terms. Someone with a $100 000 account for example, may only want to risk 1 per cent, or $1000.

⇨ using chart patterns and price to place stop losses underneath a recent price low in the case of a long trade, or above a recent price high in the case of a short trade.

⇨ using areas of support (price area through which the currency pair is unable to move lower) and resistance (price area through which the currency pair is unable to move higher).

⇨ using volatility to determine appropriate stop-loss levels far enough away from the current price to allow the trade a degree of freedom to move around, but not so far away that the stop loss, and therefore the loss of capital, is too large.

⇨ using other tools or indicators that you may develop over time, from your own experience.

How much capital can you afford to lose?

The amount of trading capital you are prepared to lose on any one trade is a matter of personal preference and personal risk tolerance. Some people are naturally more risk averse, while others have higher levels of risk tolerance. The generally accepted norms in trading are that somewhere between 1 and 5 per cent of your trading capital should be set as the maximum amount of your capital you are prepared to lose on a trade; most books and trading educators suggest 2 per cent as the amount that a trader 'should' use. Risk-averse traders might choose a lower figure, while more risk-tolerant traders may be prepared to accept a greater loss in return for potentially greater returns.

Factors other than risk tolerance will also affect the level of loss chosen, such as the accuracy of the trading system the trader is using, the profit factor of the system or methodology being used, and how often the person is trading. These topics are beyond the scope of this book, but there are a number of other great books around that deal with these concepts in greater detail for those readers interested in taking their understanding of these concepts to the next level.

Let's have a look at the effects of different percentage levels used for defining maximum capital loss on a per trade basis. If three traders all started trading forex with $10 000, all using the same trading system, their results will be radically different if only the amount of capital they are prepared to lose on each trade is varied. Trader A chooses to risk a loss of 2 per cent, or $200 ($10 000 × 2 per cent), on each trade, Trader B, chooses to risk a loss of 4 per cent, or $400 ($10 000 × 4 per cent), on each trade, and Trader C chooses to risk a loss of 8 per cent, or $800 ($10 000 × 8 per cent), on each trade. Let's assume that they have all attended a trading course and purchased a trading system or methodology with a proven track record of success and profitability over a four-year period. What Trader C has failed to grasp, however, is that despite the long-term success of the trading system, it has the potential to incur a string or run of up to six losing trades in a row, and in our example that is precisely what happens after an initial winning trade. The outcome is shown in table 9.2.

As the table shows, Trader A, who has a conservative approach to risk, has lost $666, or 6.66 per cent, of their starting capital; Trader B, who has a moderately aggressive approach to risk, has lost $1295, or 12.95 per cent of their starting capital: and risk-taking Trader C has lost $2287 or just under 23 per cent of their trading capital. Trader C will now require a 30 per cent return just to return to their original starting capital of $10 000.

Our number one priority is the preservation of our trading capital. Without capital to trade with, we can't participate in any trading activities—it's that simple. Of the three traders in our example, Trader A has clearly done the best job of preserving their capital during the string of losing trades, or draw down, that all three traders have just experienced. Having lost only a small percentage of their trading capital, this trader is well placed to keep trading the system or strategy and to take advantage of a winning run or string of winning trades when they next eventuate. Having the discipline to keep trading and applying conservative position sizing, Trader A will have also managed to maintain their confidence in the system, accepting the losses incurred as a natural part of the trading process. Trader C, on the other hand, is likely to be feeling beat-up by the market and wondering what the heck happened—and probably questioning both the soundness of the system and their ability to continue to trade it. Psychologically, Trader A remains in great shape, while Trader C is confused, dazed, and looking for all the reasons to explain away the fact that poor money management and position sizing have caused the loss of capital.

Table 9.2: effect of varying risk profiles on loss of capital from trades

Trade no.	Win or loss	Trader A		Trader B		Trader C	
		2% risk	Account $	4% risk	Account $	7% risk	Account $
			10000		10000		10000
1	W	300	10300	600	10600	1050	11050
2	L	−206	10094	−424	10176	−774	10276
3	L	−202	9892	−407	9769	−720	9556
4	L	−198	9694	−391	9405	−669	8887
5	L	−194	9500	−376	9029	−622	8265
6	L	−190	9310	−361	8668	−578	7687
7	L	−186	9124	−345	8323	−538	7149
8	W	200	9324	363	8686	550	7699
9	W	200	9524	382	9068	594	8293
10	L	−190	9334	−363	8705	−580	7713

Tip

The importance of setting stop-loss levels and clearly defining the amount of capital you are prepared to put at risk cannot be stated strongly enough. It is the most important concept in trading and one that needs to be internalised to the point where it becomes second nature for every trader serious about their success in the trading environment.

Using leverage and position sizing

Let's now apply some of the information we learned in chapter 5, and look at the use of leverage in trading forex. Remember that leverage is the act of using only a small portion of our own capital and effectively borrowing the rest from the broker or dealer to increase our exposure to a financial market.

Readers would be familiar with many of the promises of riches advertised on the internet and other media sources — 'Start trading today with only $500', 'Get up to 400 per cent leverage', and so on. While it is true that some traders have started with relatively small trading accounts and turned them into larger trading accounts, the dream of becoming a millionaire overnight turns into a nightmare when the over-use and abuse of leverage wipes out a trading account. Let's have a look at why this happens.

We will see what happens to three traders who have all decided to trade the same system, and all have the same $10 000 starting account balance. The only difference is the amount of leverage they decide to use and the impact this has on the size of their positions. We also assume for this example that of the three traders, only Trader 1 understands the importance of position sizing and money management, and has chosen to risk only 2 per cent of their trading capital on each trade, despite the potential to risk a far greater amount through the leverage available from their forex dealer firm. Traders 2 and 3, on the other hand, decide to use varying degrees of the leverage available. We will also assume that the system or trading strategy being used has a proven track record over many years and hundreds of trades, but suffers a run of six losing trades in a row when these three traders begin their quest for forex trading success. The results for the first 10 trades taken by our three traders are shown in table 9.3, which shows that all three traders made a loss of 250 pips.

Table 9.3: trade results in pips for all three traders

Trade #	Result in pips
1	150
2	−100
3	−100
4	−100
5	−100
6	−100
7	−100
8	150
9	150
10	−100
Total pips	**−250**

Trader 1 employs a position-sizing model, as discussed earlier that allows him to risk a loss of 2 per cent of his trading capital on each trade. With $10 000 capital available for trading, this means a risk of $200 per trade. The system the trader is using sets a 100 pip stop loss to determine the point at which the trade has obviously not worked out as anticipated, so Trader 1 can trade two mini lots (10 000 units) or $2 per pip (100 pips at $2 per pip = $200). With a margin requirement of 1 per cent, Trader 1 needs to lodge about $100 of his own capital for each mini lot being traded ($10 000 × 1 per cent = $100). This provides leverage of 100:1. The total margin requirement of $200 represents 2 per cent of the $10 000 trading capital available. Trader 1 has makes a very conservative use of the leverage offered, leveraging their total trading capital in this case by only 2:1 — two mini lots of 10 000, or $20 000:$10 000 of their own capital.

Tip

It is important to understand the difference between maximum leverage or available leverage and true leverage, and also to understand the leverage on each trade and the leverage on your total account.

Trader 1 has used leverage at the rate of 100:1 for the trade he is about to enter by using $200 of his trading capital as the margin on two mini forex lots (2 × $10 000 mini lots = $20 000 at 1 per cent margin = $200). He is now able to trade a $20 000 position by using $200 of his own money and effectively borrowing the balance from his forex dealing firm. He is using the available leverage rate of 100:1 on a per trade basis. His true leverage is, however, significantly less than this as he has an open position of $20 000 (two mini lots of $10 000 each) with a trading account balance of $10 000. The results for Trader 1 are shown in table 9.4.

Despite a six-trade losing streak, Trader 1 has lost just $500 or 5 per cent of his trading capital. This will require a 5.3 per cent return for him to restore his account balance to the initial amount. By adhering to the goal of capital preservation and using a conservative approach to risk management and a conservative use of the leverage on offer, he is still in the game and able to continue to participate in the forex market in order to take advantage of further trade opportunities as they arise.

Table 9.4: trade results using 2 per cent risk for Trader 1

Trade no.	Result in pips	Mini lots traded	$ per pip	Trade result $	Balance $
1	150	2	2	300	10300
2	−100	2	2	−200	10100
3	−100	2	2	−200	9900
4	−100	2	2	−200	9700
5	−100	2	2	−200	9500
6	−100	2	2	−200	9300
7	−100	2	2	−200	9100
8	150	2	2	300	9400
9	150	2	2	300	9700
10	−100	2	2	−200	9500
Total pips	−250				

Trader 2 is much more aggressive in her approach than Trader 1 and decides that because this is such a great system she is going to risk $1000 of her trading capital on each trade by trading one standard lot of $100000 or $10 per pip. With a margin requirement of 1 per cent, she will use $1000 of her own capital and 'borrow' the balance from the dealing firm. She is still using the available leverage on a per trade basis of 100:1, but her true leverage is now 10:1 because she has a $100000 position with an account balance of $10000. Her total margin requirement is 10 per cent, as she is using $1000 of her available $10000. By the time she gets to trade number 8 (see table 9.5, overleaf), the true leverage has increased to around 18:1 — her account balance has dropped to $5500 yet she is still trading one standard lot of $100000 ($100000:$5500 = 18:1). At this point she is also risking approximately 18 per cent of her available capital on the next trade ($1000 risk:$5500 available capital). Her total margin requirement is also 18 per cent, as she is using $1000 of her available $5500. The results are shown in table 9.5.

Table 9.5: trade results using a fixed $1000 risk for Trader 2

Trade no.	Result in pips	Standard lots	$ per pip	Trade result $	Balance $
1	150	1	10	1500	11 500
2	−100	1	10	−1000	10 500
3	−100	1	10	−1000	9 500
4	−100	1	10	−1000	8 500
5	−100	1	10	−1000	7 500
6	−100	1	10	−1000	6 500
7	−100	1	10	−1000	5 500
8	150	1	10	1500	7 000
9	150	1	10	1500	8 500
10	−100	1	10	−1000	7 500
Total pips	−250				

After 10 trades, Trader 2 has lost 25 per cent of her original starting capital. This will require a return of 33 per cent just to recover so she can break even.

Trader 3 is using the same system and believes it will be his sure-fire rocket to success in the forex market. He is excited about the profits the system can generate and is already planning the new boat he will buy with the money he will generate in the next few weeks. Seeing only the upside of the strategy, and with no concept of the possibility of loss or money management, he decides to trade three standard lots. His true leverage is 30:1 (three standard lots of $100 000 = $300 000:$10 000 account balance) and the available leverage is 100:1. His initial margin requirement is 30 per cent, as he is using $3000 margin of his available $10 000 account balance. The results are shown in table 9.6.

Using such an aggressive approach Trader 3 has managed to completely wipe out his account and join the ranks of many other would-be forex traders who misuse the leverage offered on their margin trading accounts. While it looks like it has taken six trades to destroy Trader 3's account, trade number six could not have been taken. There is also the possibility that a margin call would have occurred during trade number 5 when the loss on this trade exceeded the amount of money left in the Trader 3's account. With $2500 in the account, and a margin requirement of $3000 for three standard lots at 1 per cent, there is not enough money left in the account to cover the initial margin requirement.

Table 9.6: trade results using a fixed $3000 risk for Trader 3

Trade no.	Result in pips	Standard lots	$ per pip	Trade result $	Balance $
1	150	3	30	4500	14500
2	−100	3	30	−3000	11500
3	−100	3	30	−3000	8500
4	−100	3	30	−3000	5500
5	−100	3	30	−3000	2500
6	−100	3	30	−3000	−500
7	−100	0	0	0	−500
8	150	0	0	0	−500
9	150	0	0	0	−500
10	−100	0	0	0	−500
Total pips	−250				

Although some readers may think Trader 3's case is an extreme example and unlikely to occur, there are countless examples of traders blowing up their forex trading accounts through similar scenarios. They usually result from a lack of understanding of the concepts of money management and little if any knowledge of the negative effects of the dual concepts of leverage and margin.

In these examples, position sizes have not been adjusted in accordance with increases and decreases in the account balance in line with prudent money management principals. Normally, position sizes would be adjusted up and down in line with the capital available, increasing as profits are made and capital is added to the trading account, and decreasing when losses are incurred and the capital in the trading account is reduced. They are shown to highlight the need for a conservative approach to both risk management and money management, and to ensure that readers understand the detrimental affect an overly aggressive approach to trading forex can have on your financial and psychological wellbeing.

Tip

Leverage amplifies the movement in the relative prices of a currency pair by the rate of leverage being used. It magnifies both profits on winning trades and losses on trades that move against us.

Let's say you buy one standard lot of AUD/USD currency pair and it goes up by 1 per cent from 0.9900 to 1.0000—a gain of 100 pips or $1000.00 (100 pips at $10 per pip). Table 9.7 shows how leverage would affect the return on the margin used for the trade.

Table 9.7: how leverage magnifies gains

Leverage	Margin required ($)	Return (gain) on margin (%)
100:1	1 000	+100
50:1	2 000	+50
33:1	3 300	+33
20:1	5 000	+20
10:1	10 000	+10
5:1	20 000	+5
3:1	33 000	+3
1:1	100 000	+1

If the same trade goes *down* by 1 per cent from 0.9900 to 0.9801, leverage will magnify the loss. Table 9.8 shows the results.

Table 9.8: how leverage magnifies losses

Leverage	Margin required ($)	Return (loss) on margin (%)
100:1	1 000	−100
50:1	2 000	−50
33:1	3 300	−33
20:1	5 000	−20
10:1	10 000	−10
5:1	20 000	−5
3:1	33 000	−3
1:1	100 000	−1

These examples highlight the magnifying effects of leverage on your trading account and how you must know how to manage leverage and manage your risk to avoid destroying your forex trading account.

Leverage and small accounts

One of the attractions of the leverage offered when trading forex is that very small accounts can use this leverage to achieve high levels of return. As we have seen in the previous examples, the overuse and misuse of leverage can have catastrophic results for uneducated and unprepared forex traders. Let's have a look at a few examples of the effects of misusing leverage on these small accounts.

Trader Joe opens an account with $500 and decides to trade mini lots of $10 000 at $1 per pip. Having no understanding of the money management principles we have discussed here, his first trade is two mini lots of AUD/USD, with a true leverage of 40:1 ($20 000 for two mini lots: $500 account balance). He does, however, place a 30 pip stop loss under the trade. The 30 pip stop loss is reached and the trade becomes a $60 loser ($1 per pip × 2 mini lots × 30 pip stop loss), reducing his account balance to $440. He has lost 12 per cent of his trading capital ($500 − $440) and now requires a return of 14 per cent to recover his starting capital. Annoyed by this loss, Trader Joe decides to double up, and buy four mini lots on his next foray into the forex market, still with a 30 pip stop loss. His true leverage on this trade is 90:1 (4 mini lots = $40 000:$440 account balance). This trade is also a loser and it costs him $120 ($1 per pip × 4 mini lots × 30 pip stop loss), and reducing his account balance to $320 — in two trades he has lost 36 per cent of his trading capital and now needs a return of 57 per cent to return to his original $500 starting balance. The next trade of two mini lots is also a loser, reducing the account by another $60 to a balance of $260 — just over 50 per cent of the original starting amount. Trader Joe now needs a return of 100 per cent just to return to the original starting level.

These examples illustrate how and why misunderstanding and misusing leverage is the killer for the majority of people who attempt to trade forex. If harnessed correctly, leverage is a powerful tool that can magnify your gains. If not used correctly, it will wipe you out.

As well as learning everything you can about all aspects of the forex markets, capitalising your account sufficiently, trading with sensible leverage, and using strict money management rules will greatly increase your chance of success.

The use of suitable rates of leverage with proper account capitalisation will ensure losses are kept to a minimum and will enable you to adhere to the number one priority of capital preservation. Combining relatively conservative position-sizing techniques with the use of stop losses will allow you to manage your trades and your trading capital so you can survive the losing trades and remain solvent and can continue to participate in the endless stream of trading opportunities provided by the forex markets.

Chapter summary

⇨ The first step towards becoming a successful and profitable trader and building a solid foundation from which to approach the markets with a sound money management plan is setting realistic expectations in terms of time, profit and return on capital.

⇨ Most consistently successful traders are not over-night sensations but are instead long-term survivors who have a disciplined approach and a strict set of rules for trading that they adhere to without fail.

⇨ Forex trading is a game of probabilities in which there will be winning and losing trades, winning streaks and losing streaks, and periods of elation as well as periods of disappointment.

⇨ Too often, beginner traders are sold the story that with a starting balance of less than $10 000 they will be able to replace their existing weekly income or be able to fully support themselves from their trading activities within a short period of time. The reality is different.

⇨ Preserving capital is your number one priority: if you lose your capital you can't trade any more.

⇨ Stop losses, set at the start of the trade, define the point at which you will exit a trade that has moved against you and limit your losses to what you have decided you can afford to risk.

⇨ Between 1 and 5 per cent of your trading capital can be risked on each trade, depending on your personal risk preferences, trading system and net worth.

⇨ Leverage magnifies losses as well as profits: it is a double-edged sword that needs to be fully understood and respected in order to ensure your longevity in the trading environment.

⇨ Successful traders have realistic expectations.

Glossary

Glossary

American-style quotes   express the amount of US dollars needed for one unit of a foreign currency. The US dollar is quoted second and is the quote or counter currency. American-style quotes are always quoted in US dollars and cents.

arbitrage   taking advantage of price differences for the same instrument in different markets to make a profit. For example, a price difference between the same currency in the spot forex market and the futures market.

ask price   or offer price; the price sellers are willing to accept and therefore the price at which you can buy a currency.

at best   or at market; buying or selling at the current market price.

aussie   a specific forex traders' term for the Australian dollar.

balance of payments (BOP)   a measure of the payments that flow in and out of a country. The current account measures trade in goods and services, such as raw material exports and manufactured goods imports. The difference between imports and exports is referred to as the trade balance. The capital account measures flows of money for financial transactions and investment.

base currency   the first currency quoted in any forex pair.

bid   or buy price; the price buyers are prepared to pay, and therefore the price at which you can sell.

big figure   the whole dollar price of a quote without the decimal points. A currency pair trading at 109.43, for example, has a big figure of 109.

Big Mac index   a colloquial term for the purchasing power parity theory. It is based on the global availability of Big Mac hamburgers and the fact that similar inputs of domestically produced ingredients are used to produce a Big Mac. Under the PPP theory, the price of a Big Mac hamburger should in theory be the same in the base currency price the world over.

Bretton Woods Accord   or system; established in 1944, towards the end of World War II, to manage monetary and financial relations among the major industrial economies. It included the use of the gold standard to peg or fix exchange rates, and the establishment of the International Monetary Fund (IMF) and the International Bank for Reconstruction and Development (IBRD), or World Bank, to encourage and oversee global trade and reconstruction after the war.

BRIC economies   the term used to describe the emerging economies of Brazil, Russia, India and China.

broker   a firm or individual that acts as an agent between buyers and sellers; they are paid a commission on every trade.

capital account   measures money flows into and out of an economy for financial transactions and investments.

capitalisation   a measure of the size of a firm or business.

carry trade   buying a currency with a high interest rate and simultaneously selling a currency with a low interest rate. The interest rate paid on the borrowed, or sold, currency is more than offset by the interest received on the bought currency. Profit is made on the difference between the two interest rates.

central bank or reserve bank; the principal monetary authority of a nation. Central banks are usually responsible for issuing currency, controlling interest rates, overseeing the commercial banking system within a nation, and controlling the supply of money.

charting using price charts and technical indicators to arrive at trading and investment decisions.

Chicago Mercantile Exchange (CME) the regulated US futures trading exchange.

close a position or close out; to exit an open trade at either a profit or a loss. If you have a bought, or long, open position you would sell to close the position; if you have a short, or sold, open position you would buy to close the position.

consumer price index (CPI) a measure of the average price of consumer goods and services purchased by households within an economy. It measures the average change in prices paid for a constant basket of goods and services from one period to the next within the same area. It is compiled from a sample of prices for food, shelter, fuel, clothing, transportation and medical services.

core inflation rate (CPI-U) a measure of inflation that excludes food and energy components, which tend to be the most volatile and seasonal. Seasonal factors, such as drought, floods and other natural events, can cause short-term spikes in prices for these food and energy components of the index. If these sharp, short-term price increases are included in the index, they tend to inflate the value of the index in the short term. The CPI-U figure provides a smoother view of the inflation data, as it is not skewed or affected by these short term price spikes.

counter currency   or quote currency; the second currency quoted in any forex pair.

cross currency pair   also referred to as cross rate or cross; is any currency pair that does not include the US dollar on one side of the deal: examples include EUR/JPY, AUD/JPY, GBP/AUD.

cross the spread   or crossing the spread; buying at the offer price, or selling at the bid price to enter (open) or exit (close) a trade.

currency hedge   the action of locking in the value of the currency by buying or selling at the current price to avoid any further movements in exchange rates.

currency pairs   basic to forex trading. All currencies are traded against the value of another currency and so are always traded as a pair in which the value of the base currency rises and falls in value when compared to the quote currency.

currency reserve(s)   or foreign exchange reserves; amounts of various foreign currency assets held by central banks.

currency swap(s)   or swap(s); the simultaneous purchase and sale of identical amounts of one currency for another with different value dates. They allow the two parties involved in the swap to exchange aspects of a loan in one currency (the principal and interest payments) for equivalent aspects in another currency.

current account   one of two components of a country's balance of payments. The current account is the sum of the balance of trade, interest and dividends, and any foreign aid in an economy. A surplus indicates an expanding economy; a deficit indicates a contracting economy.

dealer   a retail forex firm that acts as principal, on your behalf, for your transactions in the inter-bank market.

dealing price   the price at which an order is filled.

deflation   when a country's annual inflation rate falls below zero, indicating a general decline in prices.

delivered   or delivered against; when a futures contract is held until the contract expiry date, or delivery date, when the specified amount of the commodity or currency specified in the contract must be delivered to the buyer.

delivery price   the price specified in a futures contract.

derivative   any financial security where the price is derived from the value of an underlying asset.

direct market access (DMA)   the electronic trading facilities that allow retail traders to deal directly into the market.

Electronic Broking Services (EBS)   an inter-bank dealing platform—EBS Spot Dealing System—used by the major banks and participants in the inter-bank forex market.

economic indicators   provide a general overview of conditions within an economy, and paint the broad economic picture. Economic indicators include a country's gross domestic product (GDP) and balance of trade.

emerging market currency pairs   currency pairs that are not associated with the major currency crosses from the developed economies of the world.

e-micro forex future(s)   a futures contract that is one-tenth (10 000 units) the size of a standard currency futures contract (100 000 units).

employment indicators   a measure of the structural soundness and underlying health of an economy. Low unemployment levels indicate a sound economy, while high unemployment levels indicate a struggling or slow-paced economy.

enter a trade   to buy long or sell short to open a position.

European-style quotes express the amount of currency that can be exchanged for 1 US dollar. The US dollar is quoted first and is the base currency.

Eurozone the member states of the European Community that use the euro as their single currency.

exchange rate mechanism a system introduced by the European Community in March 1979 in preparation for the introduction of the single euro currency.

exit a trade to sell out of an open long position, or buy back an open short position in order to close a trade at either a profit or a loss.

exotic currency a thinly traded currency that is illiquid and trades in low volumes. The bid/ask spread is usually wider than for the major currency pairs.

face value the full value of a contract or lot.

Federal Reserve System typically referred to as the Fed; the US central bank.

fiat money system currency that has no intrinsic value and is not backed by a commodity or any other store of value. Fiat money has value only because of government regulation.

fiscal policy the use of taxation and government spending to influence the money supply and the economy of a nation.

fixing date the date on which the details of a forward contract or swap deal are set.

floating exchange rate or floating currency; any currency that has its value determined by the forces of supply and demand in the foreign exchange market rather than a value imposed by the government.

foreign exchange see *forex*.

forex   an abbreviation for the retail foreign exchange market. Other abbreviations are retail forex, FX, margin fx, spot fx and spot.

forward contract(s)   also described as forward outrights and currency forward contracts; refers to any non-standardised contract between two parties to buy or sell a specified amount of a currency at an agreed exchange rate (called the delivery price) at an agreed future date.

forward point(s)   the adjustment factor used on a forward contract between the current value of the currency and its anticipated value at a specific time in the future.

fractional pip   an extra pip added to currency pairs that is one-tenth the value of a full pip.

fundamental analysis   the use of economic data, news announcements and other research to arrive at trading and investing decisions.

future(s)   the shortened form for a futures contract(s), which is a legally binding, standardised agreement to buy or sell a standardised commodity or financial instrument of specific quality and quantity on a specified future delivery date at a given location.

gold standard   a monetary standard where a unit of the currency is exchangeable for a specified amount of gold. The gold standard is no longer used as the major world currencies are free floating and have their values determined by supply and demand on the world currency markets. The only exception is the Swiss franc, which is partly backed by gold.

government securities   bonds, treasury notes and other debt instruments issued by a government to finance its borrowings.

gross domestic product (GDP)   a measure of all the goods and services produced in an economy within a 12-month period. GDP is a good measure of the overall size of an economy and is an effective way of comparing different economies around the world.

G10 currency pairs   the currency pairs that contain the currencies of the G10 countries.

headline figure(s)   the main number resulting from a report or survey and the one that grabs the attention of traders and the media, and makes the headlines. An example is the quarterly consumer price index (CPI).

hedge   or hedging; see *currency hedging*.

hitting the bid   selling at the bid, or buy, price.

hitting the offer   buying at the offer, or ask, price.

Ifo Survey   a monthly survey conducted in Germany that asks German firms about the current business climate and their expectations for the next six months.

inflation   a general rise in the prices of goods and services in an economy over time. See also *CPI*.

inflation indicators   used to gauge the level of price stability within an economy. They include the consumer price index (CPI) and the producer price index (PPI).

Institute for Supply Management (ISM) Index   a monthly index in the US that measures the activity of nationwide purchasing managers in the manufacturing and industrial sectors.

inter-bank market   the trading of currencies between the large banks and other financial institutions.

International Monetary Fund (IMF)   an international organisation of member countries that aims for cooperation on exchange rates and other monetary issues between members.

International Money Market (IMM)   developed by traders at the Chicago Mercantile Exchange (CME) in the early 1970s to allow them to trade currency and interest rate futures.

lagging economic indicators   supply data and information on an event or events that have already happened, usually some time after the event. The unemployment rate is an example of a lagging indicator as it responds slowly to changes that have already occurred within an economy and the information and numbers are often reported several months after the changes have already taken place.

law of one price   see *purchasing power parity*.

leading economic indicators   attempt to anticipate future events based on past data, so they tend to change before the economy changes. The stock market is often seen as a leading economic indicator as it tends to begin to rise before an economy comes out of a recession and begins to expand, and often falls in value before an economy goes into a recession or period of economic contraction.

leverage   sometimes referred to as leverage up; the use of margin to increase the size of trades you are able to make by borrowing from your dealing firm.

limit order   an entry order to buy a currency pair below the prevailing market price or to sell a currency pair above the prevailing market price. Limit orders can also be used as take profit orders once a trade has been entered either above the prevailing market price, for a long position, or below the prevailing market price, for a short position.

liquidity   the volume of transactions. The more liquid a currency pair is, the more buyers and sellers are participating in the market, and the easier it is to enter and exit trades.

long position   or going long; buying a currency pair in anticipation of a further increase in the price of the base currency.

lot size   the amount of a forex currency pair you can deal in. Standard lots are for 100 000 units; mini lots are for 10 000 units; and micro lots are for 1000 units.

maintenance margin   or variation margin; the margin, or amount of money, that you must have in your trading account to ensure you do not receive a margin call.

majors   the most commonly traded currency pairs, usually involving the US dollar on one side of the currency pair.

margin call   when the mark to market loss on a trade exceeds the amount of money in your trading account. A margin call will require you to put extra cash into your trading account or close a position or positions in order to ensure sufficient margin is maintained in your account to cover the margin requirement of any open positions.

market maker(s)   a firm in the retail forex market that maintains bid/ask prices and is willing and able to deal with clients at these publicly quoted prices. These prices may not always reflect the actual prices trading in the inter-bank market. A market maker will often take the other side of a client's trade.

market order(s)   any order to buy or sell a currency at the prevailing market price.

mark-to-market   recording the value of open positions and total account value on a daily basis to calculate profits and losses and margin requirements.

monetary policy   used by a country's central bank to control the money supply in an economy, through the use of interest rate policies. Monetary policy may be described as expansionary or contractionary, depending on the effect it aims to have on the economy.

money supply   the total amount of money available in an economy at any time.

naked intervention   or unsterilised intervention; the direct buying or selling of a country's currency by its central bank. Naked intervention leads to changes in the money supply.

net exports   see *trade balance*.

net position   balance of all open long positions minus all open short positions.

nominal interest rate(s)   the current interest rate, not adjusted for the effects of inflation.

non-dealing desk (NDD) firm(s)   a retail forex firm that offers direct access to the market for clients through electronic dealing platforms. The firm acts as the principal for a client in the inter-bank market, but it does not take the other side of the client's trades, in the way a market maker would.

non-deliverable forward (NDF)   a short-term, cash-settled currency transaction that takes place directly between two counterparties.

novation   the operation of the clearing house in the futures market whereby the clearing house assumes the role of buyer against the seller and seller against the buyer to ensure that the counterparties to a trade are never exposed to default risk by the other party.

NYLON   the spot forex trading times when both London and New York are open simultaneously.

offer price   see *ask price*.

official dollarisation   the use of the US dollar by other countries as an accepted form of currency, even though they have their own currency.

official interest rates   interest rates set by a nation's central bank.

offsetting   a process used by market makers to reduce their risk in the market by buying the equivalent amount of a currency that a client or clients are short, or selling the equivalent amount if they are long.

open market operation(s) the buying and selling of government securities by a nation's central bank in order to control money supply and short-term interest rates.

open long position a position bought in anticipation of future currency price increases.

open position any current trade where the trader is either long or short.

open short position a position sold in anticipation of future currency price falls.

over the counter (OTC) the direct trading of any financial instrument or security between two parties, rather than through the use of a regulated exchange.

peg rate or pegged (currency); operates when a currency's exchange rate is fixed to the value of another stronger, or more widely accepted, currency, such as the euro or the US dollar.

percentage in point see *pip*.

performance bond also called a security deposit; an initial good-faith deposit required by a broker or dealer to open a trade when the client is using a margin account.

petro-currency a term used to describe the Canadian dollar because of its close correlation with the price of oil and other energy commodities.

pip an abbreviation for percentage in point or price index point, and it is the smallest price move a spot currency pair can make.

producer price index (PPI) a measure of the average change in selling prices received by domestic producers within an economy. Previously called the wholesale price index, it is an index of wholesale price changes that is seen as an indicator of potential future retail price changes.

profit target a predetermined price at which you will exit a trade for a profit.

purchasing power parity (PPP)   the theory that the price of a product in one country should be equal to the price of the same product in another country when converted to a common currency.

quote currency   see *counter currency*.

real interest rate differential theory   the theory that a nation's interest rate is the major determinant of exchange rate movements. It suggests that currencies should appreciate in value in countries where interest rates are relatively high or rising, while currencies should depreciate in value in countries where interest rates are low or falling.

Repurchase agreement   also called repos or sale and purchase agreements; a contract that gives the seller the right to buy back the asset at a specified price and date. In the forex market repos are used by dealers in government securities on an over-night basis. The dealer sells a government security, such as a treasury bond, to an investor, with an agreement to buy it back again the next day. Repos are effectively a form of short-term borrowing for dealers in government securities.

requote   occurs when the original price seen on the dealing platform is amended by the market maker between the time a trader's order is placed and when the order is filled.

reserve currency   any of the major currencies held in a large quantity by central banks and other financial institutions as part of their currency reserves. Traditionally, the US dollar has been the major global reserve currency, along with the British pound, the Japanese yen and the Swiss franc. The euro is now the second-largest reserve currency.

reserve requirement   or cash reserve ratio, is a requirement in many countries that commercial banks and other financial institutions that hold customer cash deposits hold a percentage of these deposits and account balances on deposit at the central bank.

resting order(s)   or a pending order; any stop or limit order that has not been filled yet at the price specified

retail forex   the electronic trading of foreign exchange through online dealing platforms with dealing firms and market makers by small traders and speculators.

Reuters   an inter-bank dealing platform.

reverse repo   or matched sale; when the country's central bank sells repos. The result is a temporary draining of funds from the banking system, which pushes up interest rates and increases the price of the country's currency on foreign exchange markets.

rollover   or roll; means extending the settlement date of an open spot forex position by closing an open position at the end of the day and immediately reopening it at the opening of the next day. Rollover is executed automatically in your account by the forex dealing firm.

safe-haven currency   a currency that is perceived by investors to offer stability during times of economic or geo-political crisis. Favoured safe-haven currencies include the Swiss franc, Japanese yen, US dollar and euro.

S&P 500   short for Standard & Poors 500, which is an index of 500 leading stocks in the US.

secondary currency   a term sometimes used to describe the quote or counter currency.

settlement date   the date on which a contract must be settled in cash or delivered.

share price index (SPI)   a futures contract based on an index of stocks. In Australia the SPI 200 futures contract is based on the index of the leading 200 stocks on the Australian Securities Exchange.

short selling   or a short position; selling a currency pair in anticipation of a further fall in the price of the base currency. Profit is made when the position is bought back at a lower price.

slippage the difference between the price you expect to enter or exit a trade and the actual price you receive when the trade is entered.

Smithsonian Agreement an agreement reached in December 1971 by the G10 countries to maintain fixed exchange rates without the backing of gold.

smoothed index an index where the raw data has been adjusted for other variables such as time, inflation, seasonal influences or other factors.

spot forex also known as spot, spot market and spot fx; a colloquial name for the retail forex market.

spread the difference between the bid and the ask price.

sterilised intervention offsetting the impact on other areas of the economy of a nation's central bank intervening in the currency markets. The bank sells or buys government securities to offset the money either generated through the sale of the currency, or spent buying the currency.

stop order an entry order to buy above the prevailing market price or sell below the prevailing market price. Also used as stop-loss orders once a trade is entered either below the prevailing market price in a long trade, or above the prevailing market price in a short trade.

stop loss a preset price point at which a trade will be exited if it moves in the opposite direction to the one anticipated.

swap(s) see *currency swaps*.

technical analysis the use of price charts, indicators, patterns and algorithms to arrive at trading decisions.

tick value the minimum price move of a futures contract.

trade balance   or net exports; a measure of the difference between exports from and imports into an economy

trade deficit   or trade gap; occurs when an economy imports more than it exports. A deficit is generally considered unfavourable for both the economy and its currency.

trade surplus   when an economy exports more than it imports; a surplus is generally considered favourable for both the economy and its currency.

trade weighted index (TWI)   the value of a country's currency in relation to a basket of currencies of that country's major trading partners. Each currency within the index is given a weight according to the amount of trade the country does with each other country.

unwind a trade   to exit a trade or open position.

variation margin   or maintenance margin; the extra margin required by the clearing house and the brokerage firm if the mark-to-market loss on an open position(s) exceeds the balance in a trader's account.

World Bank   the commonly used name for the International Bank for Reconstruction and Development (IBRD) formed under the Bretton Woods Accord at the end of World War II.

yield   the return on investment.

ZEW survey   a monthly survey conducted in Germany of financial analysts from finance, trading and investment firms, predominantly in Germany.

Index

Printed and bound by CPI Group (UK) Ltd, Croydon, CR0 4YY

26/03/2025

14648037-0001